AF226051

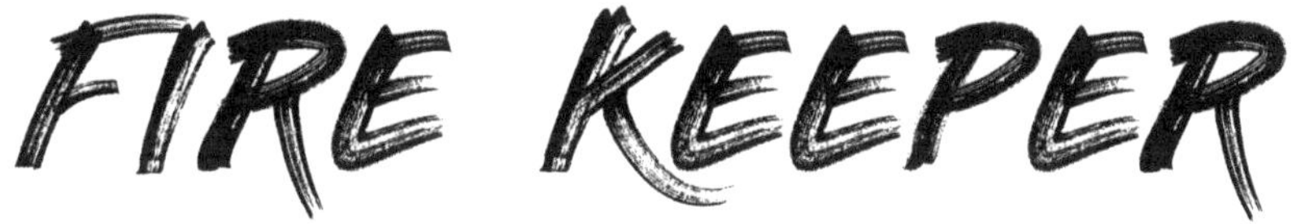

FIRE KEEPER

SELF-EXPRESSION, REIMAGINED

Jessica Blue

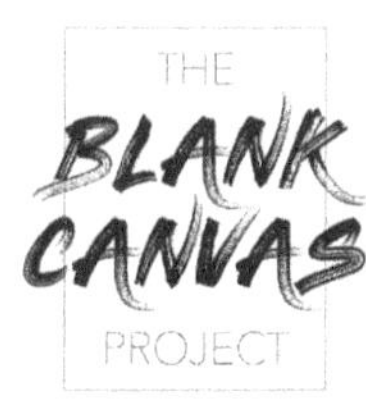

VANCOUVER, CANADA

Author: Jessica Blue
Publisher: The Blank Canvas Project

blankcanvasproject.ca
Instagram: @selfexpression.reimagined

Firekeeper / Jessica Blue — 1st ed.
ISBN 978-1-7779694-0-0

For all of you who have been made to believe

(either by yourself or others)

that you're not creative,

this book is for you.

May you find the courage to create anyway.

CONTENTS

WHAT IF I HAD THE ABILITY
TO LIGHT AND FUEL
MY OWN INNER FIRE?
WHAT IF I FOCUSED
INTENTIONAL DAILY EFFORT
ON STOKING IT AND
KEEPING IT LIT?
WHAT WOULD I BE
CAPABLE OF CREATING
IN THIS WORLD WITH THAT
LEVEL OF SELF DEVOTION
AT MY CORE?

INTRODUCTION

Have you ever had an idea, tried to avoid it because it scared the shit out of you, and then inevitably surrendered to it because it was so persistent?

Fire Keeper started as an idea for a 100-day Instagram post challenge. I've never been much of a content creator, or opinion sharer for that matter, and felt called to start somewhere. So from April to July 2021, I wrote a post a day, with only a few minor slips (hey, nobody's perfect!). Around the half way mark, the vision for the book appeared.

This book is a love letter to my humanity. Each page is an exploration of the corners of my Self that I've long kept hidden, the patterns of behaviour I'd rather not think about - all out in the open in an effort to heal, grow and ignite my inner fire. Each section title encompasses both the light and the dark facets of my Essence, my true Self.

Open flame has long served as a spiritual symbol, as well as played a central role in human survival. Similarly, the person tasked with keeping the sacred fire alight held a sacred role within ancient cultures. A perpetual flame provided hot coals for the kindling of other fires in the community.

Everyone is creative. Some of us have simply forgotten over time or been made to believe otherwise. So if you're not creating, what has you stuck? I've left a few blank pages at the end, for you to write down your own inevitable realizations. Don't think about the words too hard – allow them to flow intuitively so you can get to the important part of creating.

Become your own creative fire keeper, then watch as that fire becomes the kindling for others.

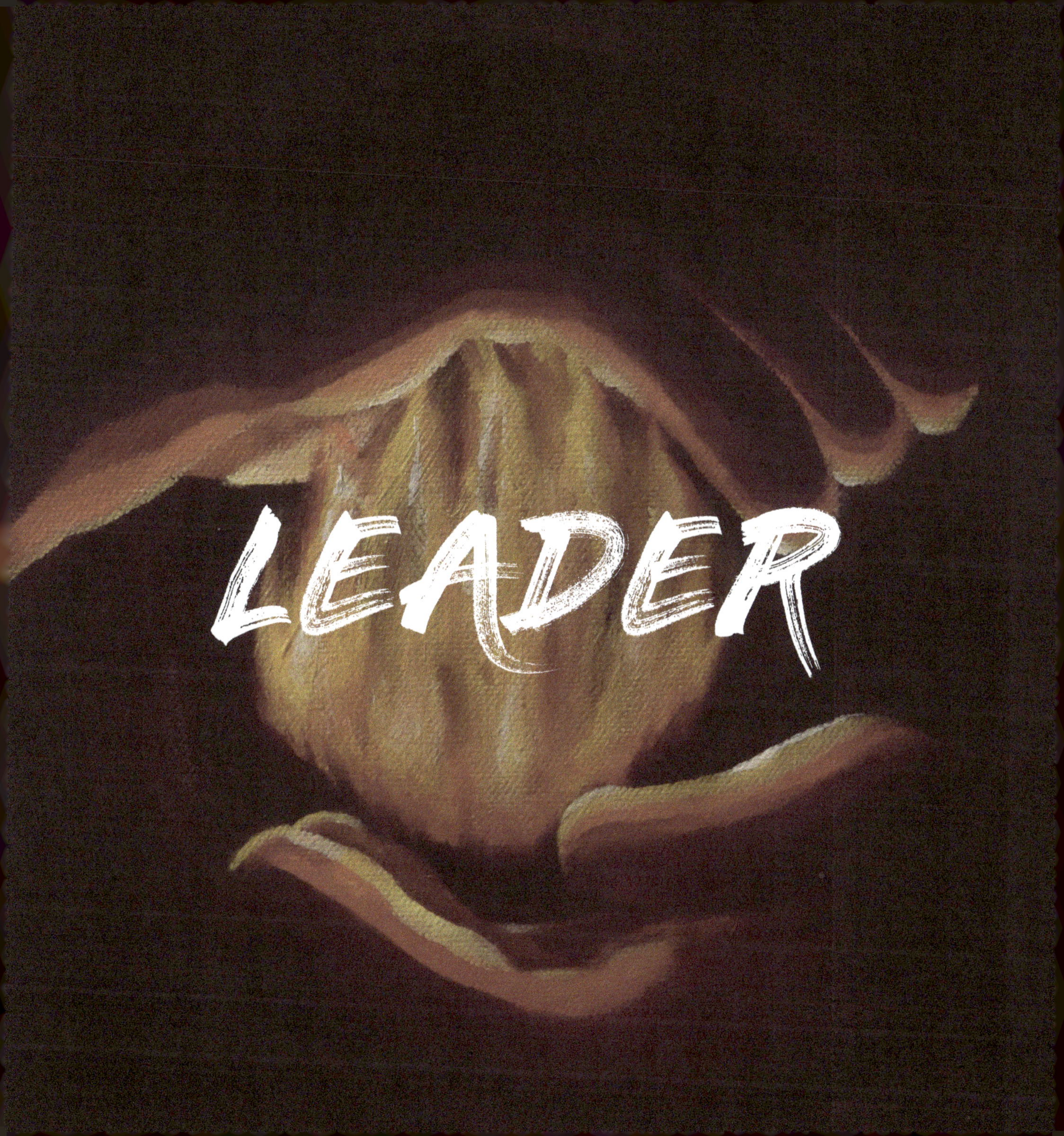
LEADER

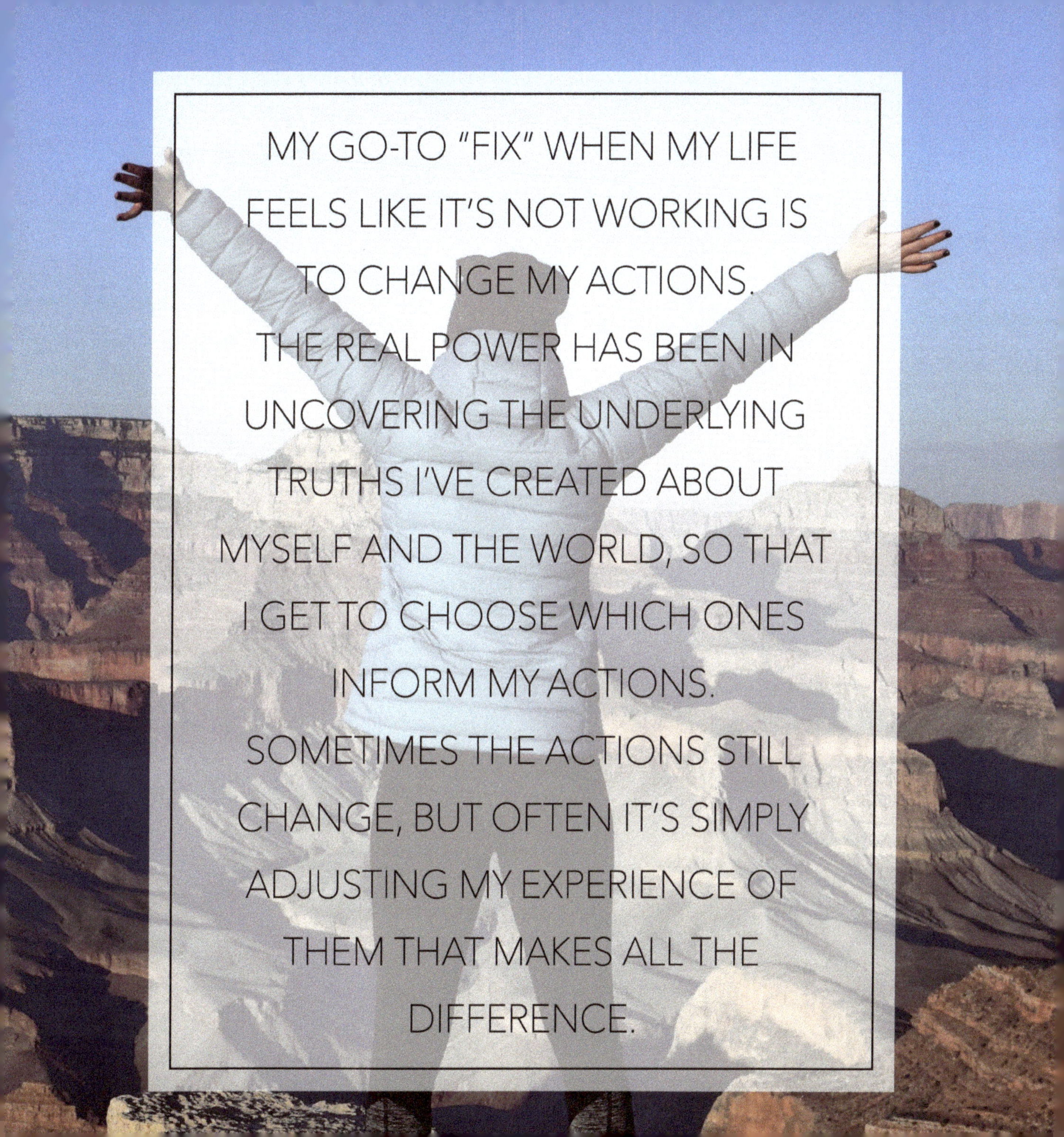

MY GO-TO "FIX" WHEN MY LIFE FEELS LIKE IT'S NOT WORKING IS TO CHANGE MY ACTIONS. THE REAL POWER HAS BEEN IN UNCOVERING THE UNDERLYING TRUTHS I'VE CREATED ABOUT MYSELF AND THE WORLD, SO THAT I GET TO CHOOSE WHICH ONES INFORM MY ACTIONS. SOMETIMES THE ACTIONS STILL CHANGE, BUT OFTEN IT'S SIMPLY ADJUSTING MY EXPERIENCE OF THEM THAT MAKES ALL THE DIFFERENCE.

THERE'S A PHILOSOPHICAL NOTION
THAT I LIKE THAT SAYS WE'RE NOT OUR
THOUGHTS, BUT RATHER THE BEING
WHO IS OBSERVING AND ANALYZING
OUR THOUGHTS.
RECENTLY, I'VE BEEN EXPLORING THE
IDEA OF THREADS OF IDENTITY - AN
ANALOGY FOR THE TRAITS AND
PATTERNS THAT MAKE UP
WHO I AM AS A PERSON.
AND THAT GOT ME THINKING,
WHAT IF I'M NOT ACTUALLY THE
THREADS OF IDENTITY THEMSELVES, BUT
RATHER THE BEING WHO IS OBSERVING
AND WEAVING THE THREADS INSTEAD?

SOMETIMES THE THING THAT I
WANT ISN'T IN ALIGNMENT WITH
MY GREATER OVERALL
COMMITMENTS TO MYSELF.
WHEN THIS HAPPENS, I HAVE TO
REMIND MYSELF OF WHY I MADE
THE COMMITMENTS IN THE FIRST
PLACE AND TRUST THAT IT WILL BE
WORTH IT IN THE LONG RUN.
THIS IS RARELY A RESISTANCE-FREE
PROCESS AND SOMETIMES I STILL
CHOOSE THE SHORT TERM
REWARD.

I'VE BEEN SUBCONSCIOUSLY
LIVING MY LIFE BASED ON
A MOTTO OF
"DON'T TAKE MORE THAN I NEED."
WHICH SOUNDS GREAT ON THE
SURFACE, EXCEPT THAT IT HAS
MANIFESTED AS ME NEVER
ACTUALLY GETTING WHAT I NEED
BECAUSE I'M TOO BUSY TRYING TO
NOT CROSS THE ARBITRARY LINE
OF "TOO MUCH."
SO I'M CHANGING THE NARRATIVE:
"I AM WORTH OF ABUNDANCE"

I'M WARY OF INTIMACY LATELY.
NOT SO MUCH WITH LONG
STANDING CONNECTIONS,
BUT WITH NEW ONES.
I THOUGHT MAYBE I WAS
BAD AT IT, IN SOME WAY.
BUT I THINK IT'S MERELY THE
WALLS I HAVE UP TO PROTECT
MY SENSITIVE HEART.
I'M LEARNING A BABY DEER LEVEL
OF TRUST IN MYSELF AND
LEANING ON THE INTIMACY
I'VE ALREADY CREATED AS
POSITIVE PROOF.

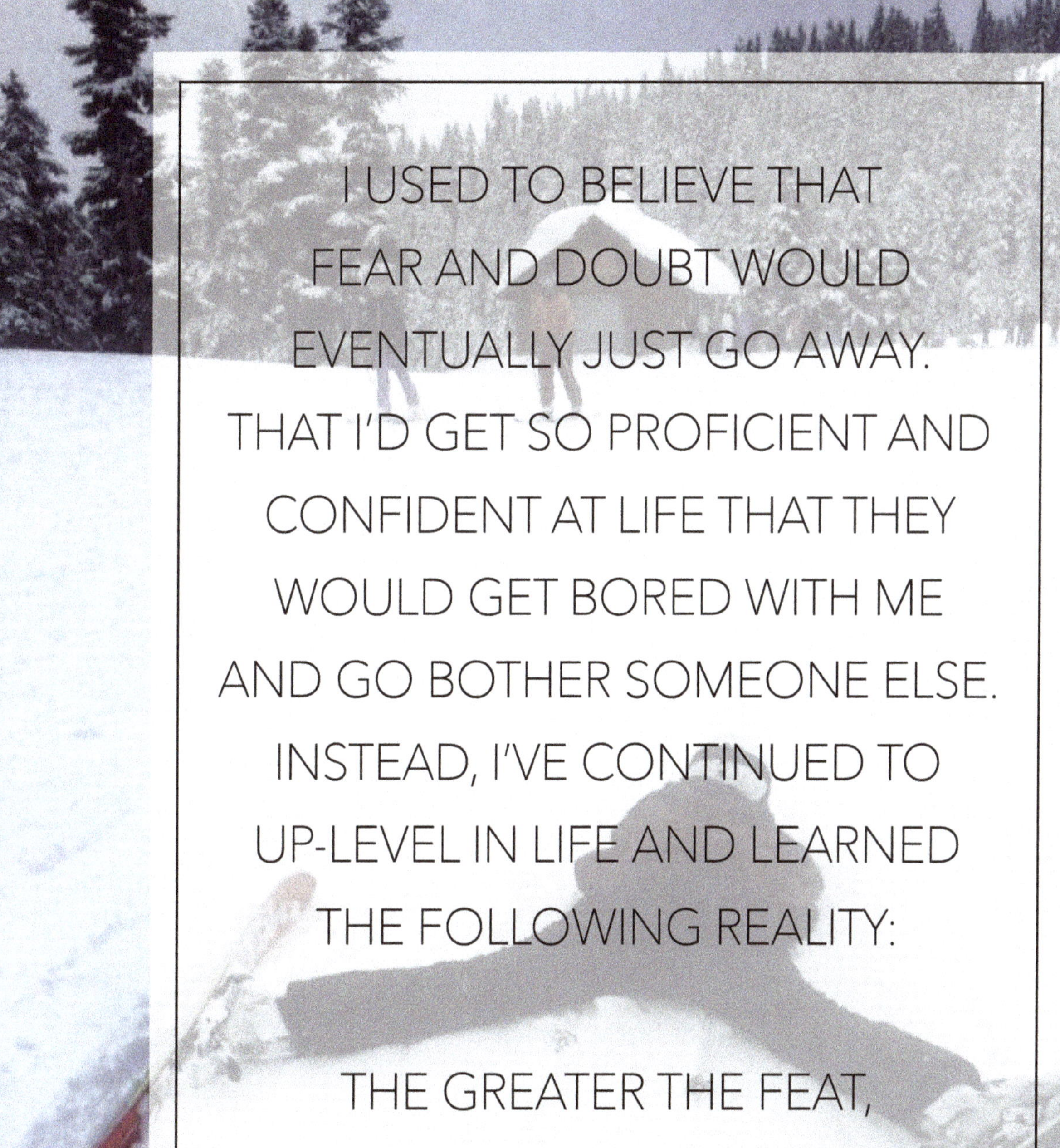
I USED TO BELIEVE THAT
FEAR AND DOUBT WOULD
EVENTUALLY JUST GO AWAY.
THAT I'D GET SO PROFICIENT AND
CONFIDENT AT LIFE THAT THEY
WOULD GET BORED WITH ME
AND GO BOTHER SOMEONE ELSE.
INSTEAD, I'VE CONTINUED TO
UP-LEVEL IN LIFE AND LEARNED
THE FOLLOWING REALITY:

THE GREATER THE FEAT,
THE GREATER THE FEAR.

SPIRITUALITY IS A HUGE PART
OF MY LIFE,
PARTICULARLY IN THE PAST YEAR.
THERE IS A MAGIC AND
A RICHNESS TO IT THAT
TRANSCENDS LOGIC.
PRACTICES THAT I USED TO
REFER TO AS 'FLUFFY', SUCH AS
ORACLE CARDS OR JOURNALLING,
HAVE BECOME POWERFUL TOOLS
FOR HONING MY LISTENING
AND LEARNING TO
TRUST THE UNIVERSE.

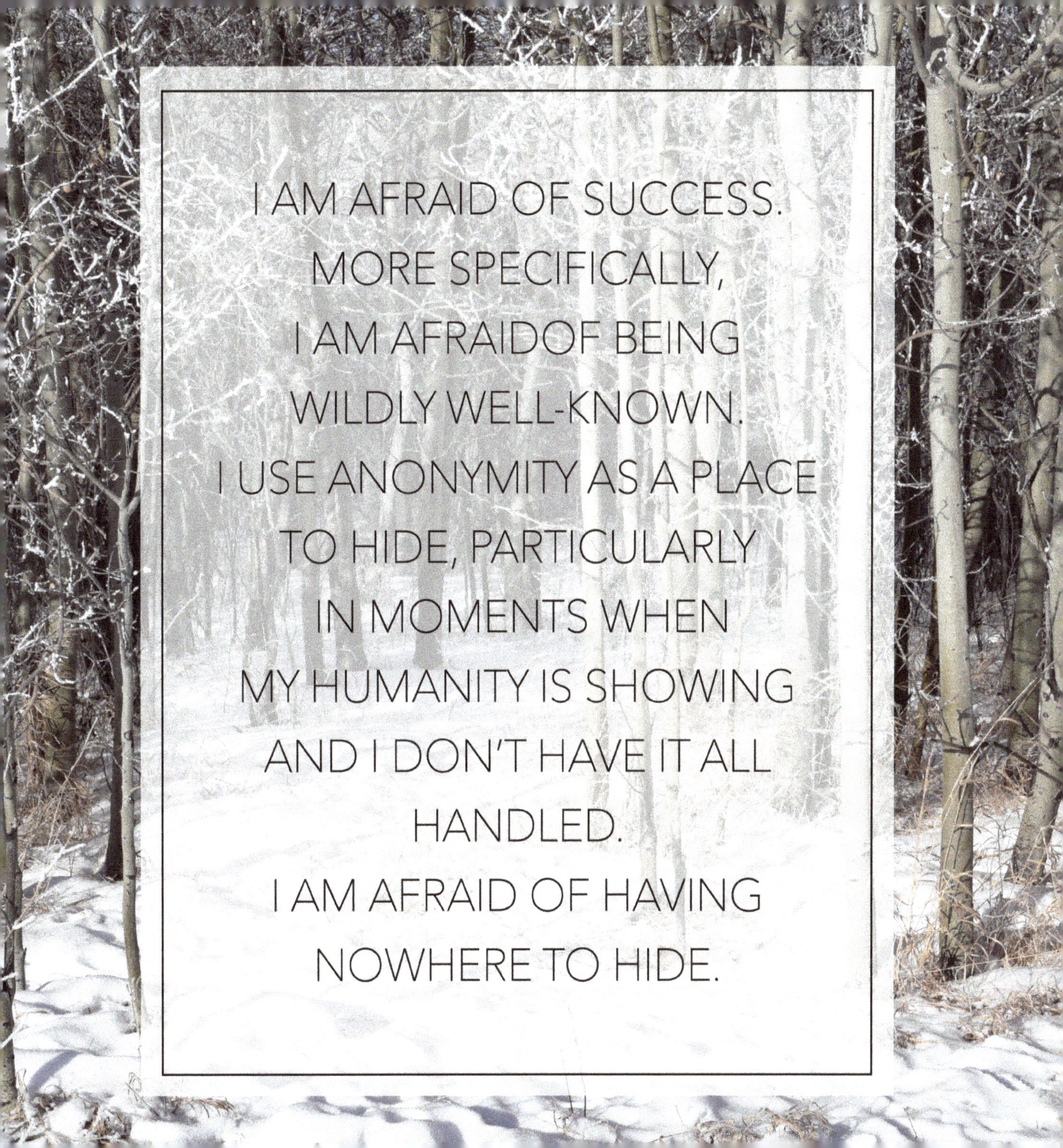
I AM AFRAID OF SUCCESS.
MORE SPECIFICALLY,
I AM AFRAIDOF BEING
WILDLY WELL-KNOWN.
I USE ANONYMITY AS A PLACE
TO HIDE, PARTICULARLY
IN MOMENTS WHEN
MY HUMANITY IS SHOWING
AND I DON'T HAVE IT ALL
HANDLED.
I AM AFRAID OF HAVING
NOWHERE TO HIDE.

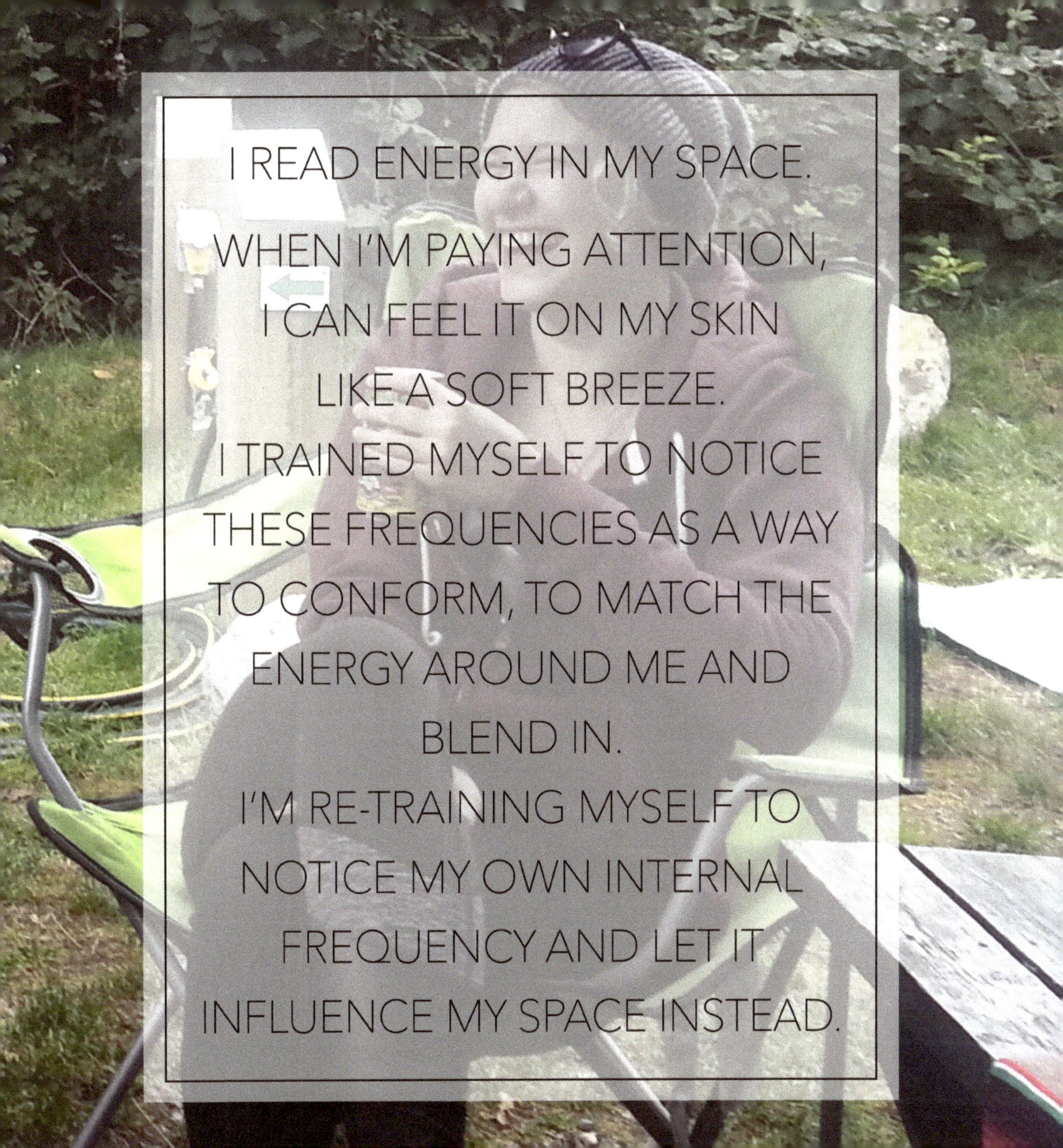

I READ ENERGY IN MY SPACE.
WHEN I'M PAYING ATTENTION,
I CAN FEEL IT ON MY SKIN
LIKE A SOFT BREEZE.
I TRAINED MYSELF TO NOTICE
THESE FREQUENCIES AS A WAY
TO CONFORM, TO MATCH THE
ENERGY AROUND ME AND
BLEND IN.
I'M RE-TRAINING MYSELF TO
NOTICE MY OWN INTERNAL
FREQUENCY AND LET IT
INFLUENCE MY SPACE INSTEAD.

THE IMPACT I'D LIKE TO HAVE IN THE
WORLD IS SOMETHING THAT I THINK
(AND WORRY) ABOUT REGULARLY.
THE THING IS, IN MY EXPERIENCE IMPACT
IS RARELY DISCERNIBLE OR WITHIN MY
CONTROL. UNLESS SOMEONE EXPLICITLY
TELLS ME THE IMPACT I'M HAVING ON
THEM, IT'S EASY TO FORGET THAT
I'M HAVING ONE AT ALL TIMES
WHETHER I'M AWARE OF IT OR NOT.
I TRY AND THINK ABOUT IT IN TERMS OF
INSPIRATION: IF SOMEONE WERE INSPIRED
BY MY ACTIONS OR WORDS TODAY, WHAT
WOULD I LIKE THAT TO LOOK LIKE?

THERE ARE SO MANY ATROCITIES BEING
BROADCAST DAILY AT AN INCREDIBLY HIGH
FREQUENCY AND MY NATURAL RESPONSE
FROM MY PRIVILEGED STANDING IN LIFE
IS TO NUMB OR AVOID ALL OF IT.
THAT IS AN OPTION FOR ME, ONE THAT
WOULD BE VERY EASY TO CHOOSE.
AND I DO CHOOSE THAT SOMETIMES.
INSTEAD THERE IS A CALL FORWARD TO
USE THAT SPACIOUSNESS I ALREADY
POSSESS THROUGH PRIVILEGE TO TAKE
ACTION SO THAT THE PEOPLE MORE
DIRECTLY AFFECTED BY THESE EVENTS GET
TO EXPERIENCE SOME SPACE TOO.

I CONSISTENTLY STRUGGLE TO OBEY MY

OWN AUTHORITY WHICH MEANS I ALSO

CONSISTENTLY GET IN MY OWN WAY

(USUALLY OUT OF FEAR).

AS A WAY TO AVOID THE DISCOMFORT

OF THIS, I LEAN TOWARDS STRUCTURES

THAT HAVE TRADITIONAL HIERARCHIES

OF LEADERSHIP TO DEFER TO.

THIS STRATEGY WORKS UNTIL I COME UP

AGAINST AN AREA OF MY LIFE WHERE

THERE IS NO ONE ELSE TO DEFER TO

BUT ME AND I GET TO PRACTICE BEING A

LEADER TO THE PART OF ME

THAT GETS IN THE WAY.

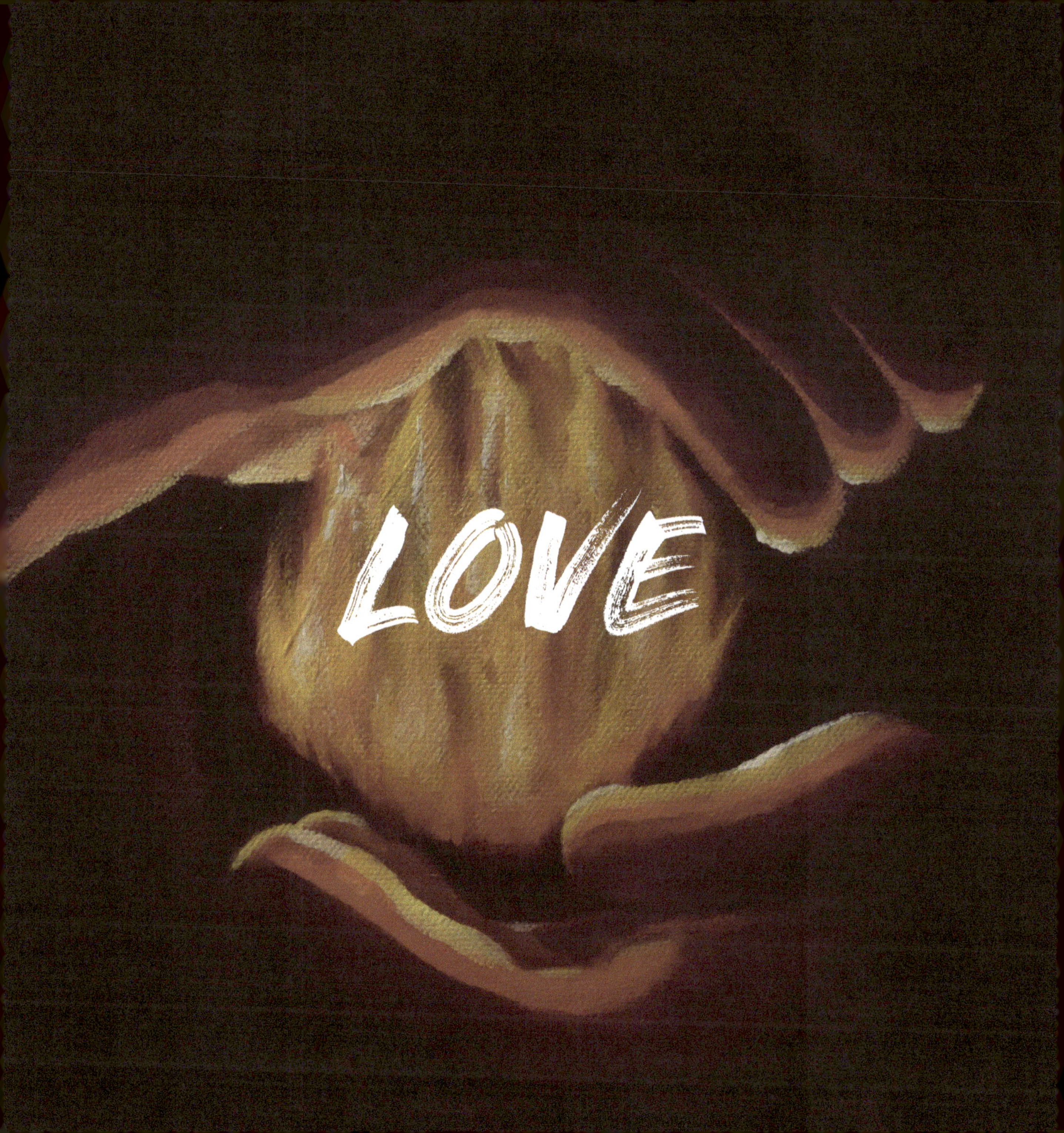
LOVE

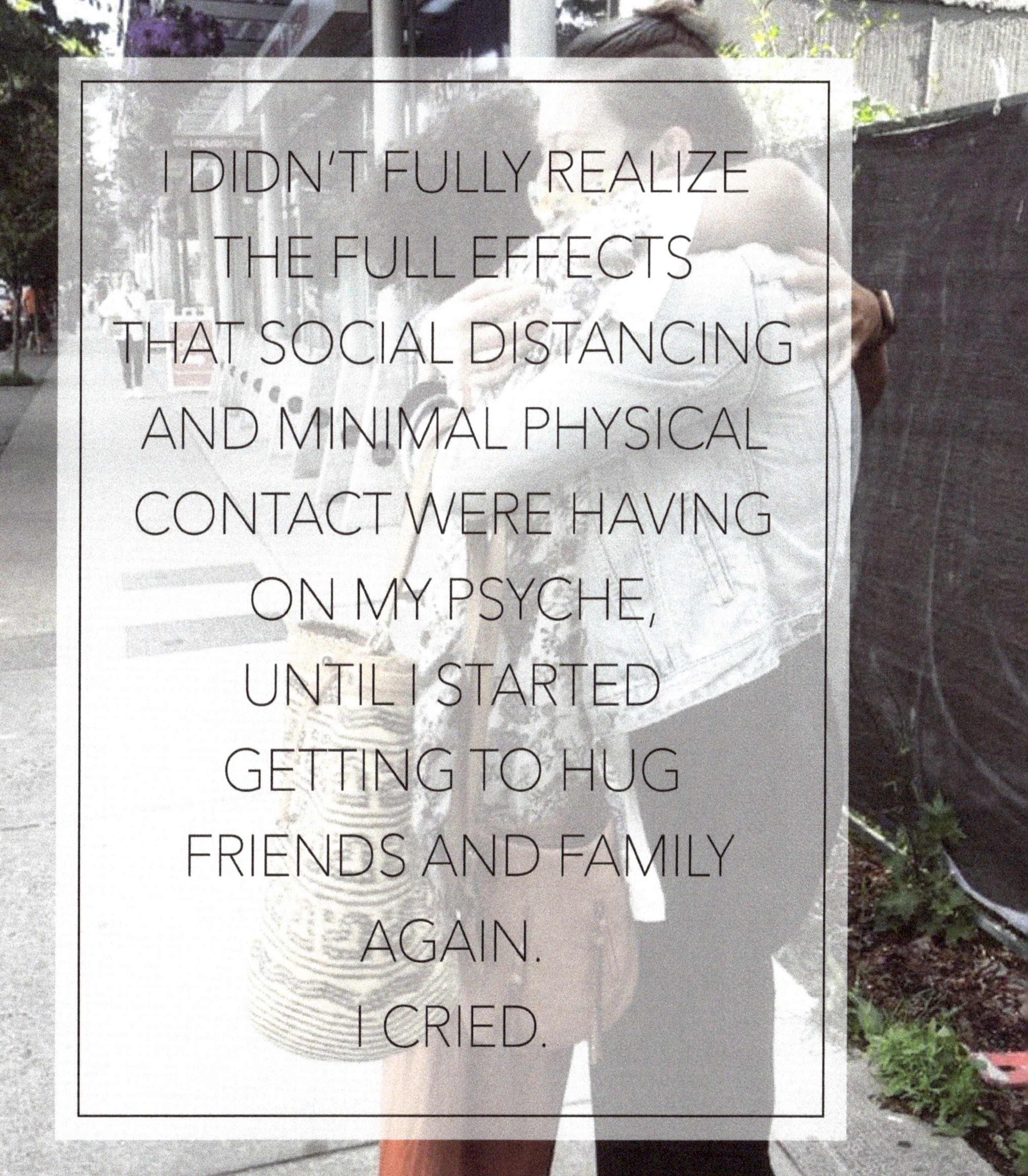
I DIDN'T FULLY REALIZE
THE FULL EFFECTS
THAT SOCIAL DISTANCING
AND MINIMAL PHYSICAL
CONTACT WERE HAVING
ON MY PSYCHE,
UNTIL I STARTED
GETTING TO HUG
FRIENDS AND FAMILY
AGAIN.
I CRIED.

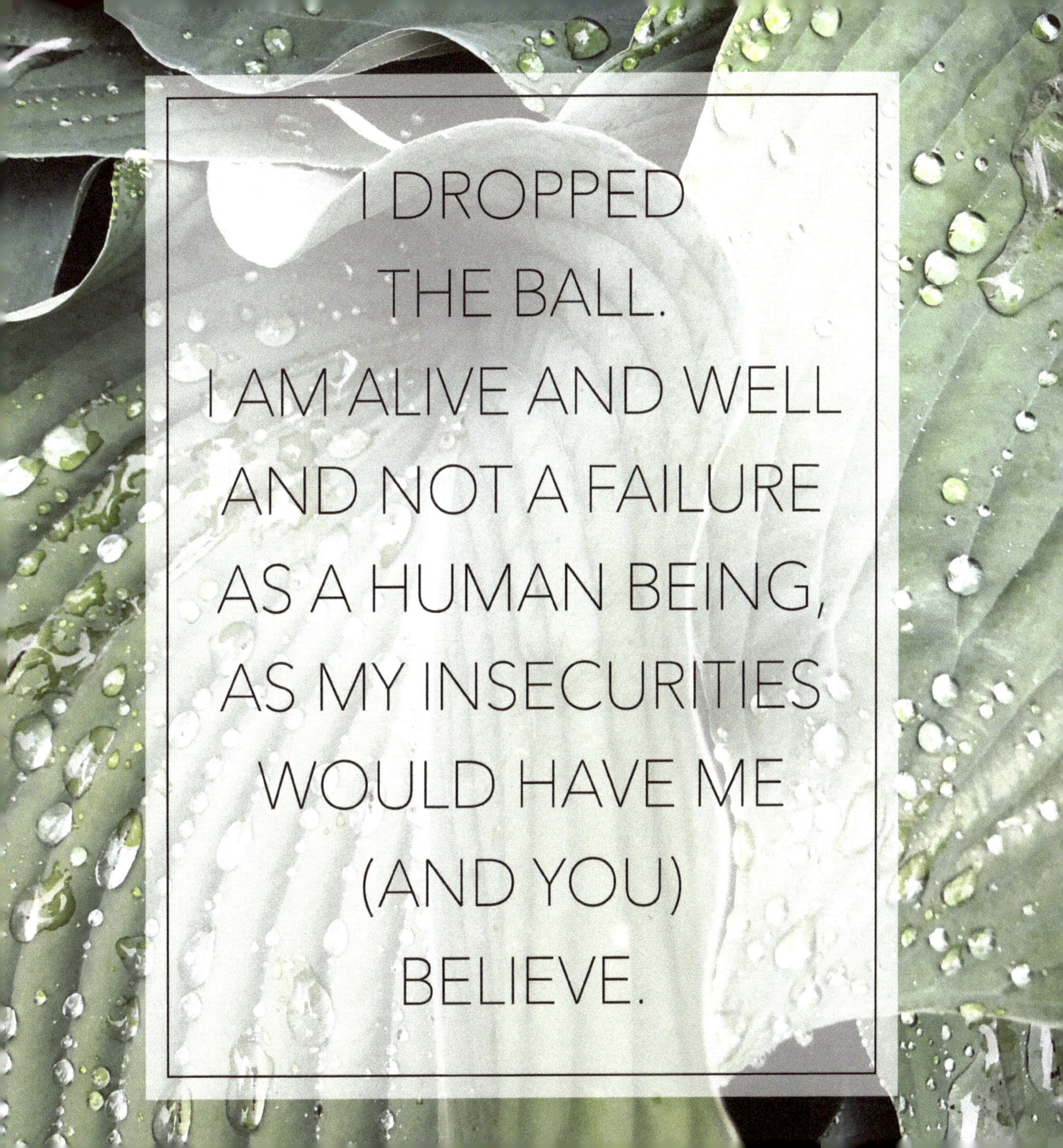
I DROPPED
THE BALL.
I AM ALIVE AND WELL
AND NOT A FAILURE
AS A HUMAN BEING,
AS MY INSECURITIES
WOULD HAVE ME
(AND YOU)
BELIEVE.

MY HEART IS TENDER.
I HAVE STRONG SOMATIC (BODY)
RESPONSES TO MOST THINGS,
AND UP UNTIL RECENTLY I SPENT
A LOT OF ENERGY SHUTTING
THEM DOWN.
I'M LEARNING TO EXPAND MY
WINDOW OF TOLERANCE
AS WELL AS GROUND IN THE
MOMENT, RATHER THAN
SIMPLY SHUT OFF.
SOME DAYS THAT'S HARDER TO
DO THAN OTHERS.

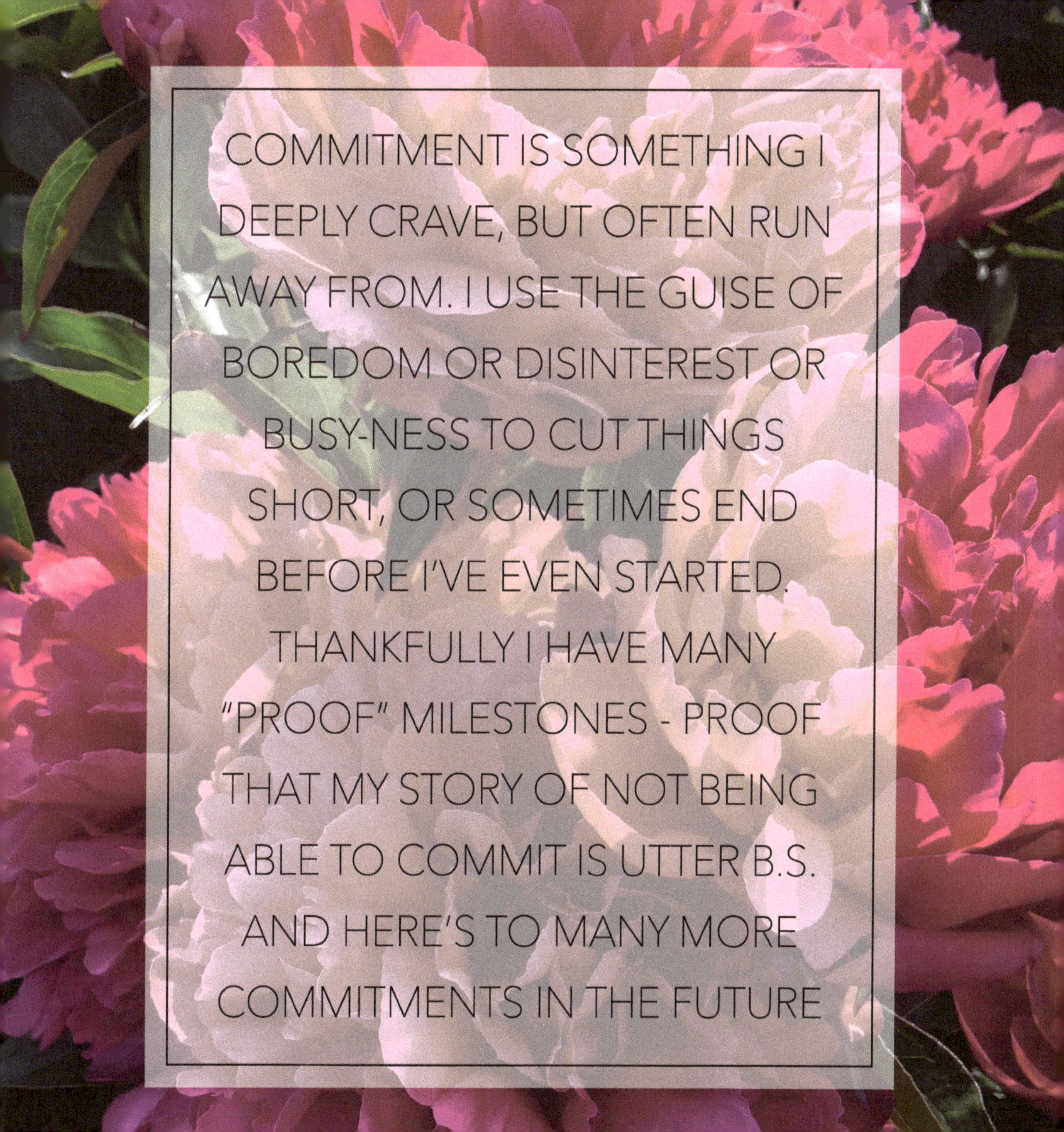

COMMITMENT IS SOMETHING I DEEPLY CRAVE, BUT OFTEN RUN AWAY FROM. I USE THE GUISE OF BOREDOM OR DISINTEREST OR BUSY-NESS TO CUT THINGS SHORT, OR SOMETIMES END BEFORE I'VE EVEN STARTED. THANKFULLY I HAVE MANY "PROOF" MILESTONES - PROOF THAT MY STORY OF NOT BEING ABLE TO COMMIT IS UTTER B.S. AND HERE'S TO MANY MORE COMMITMENTS IN THE FUTURE

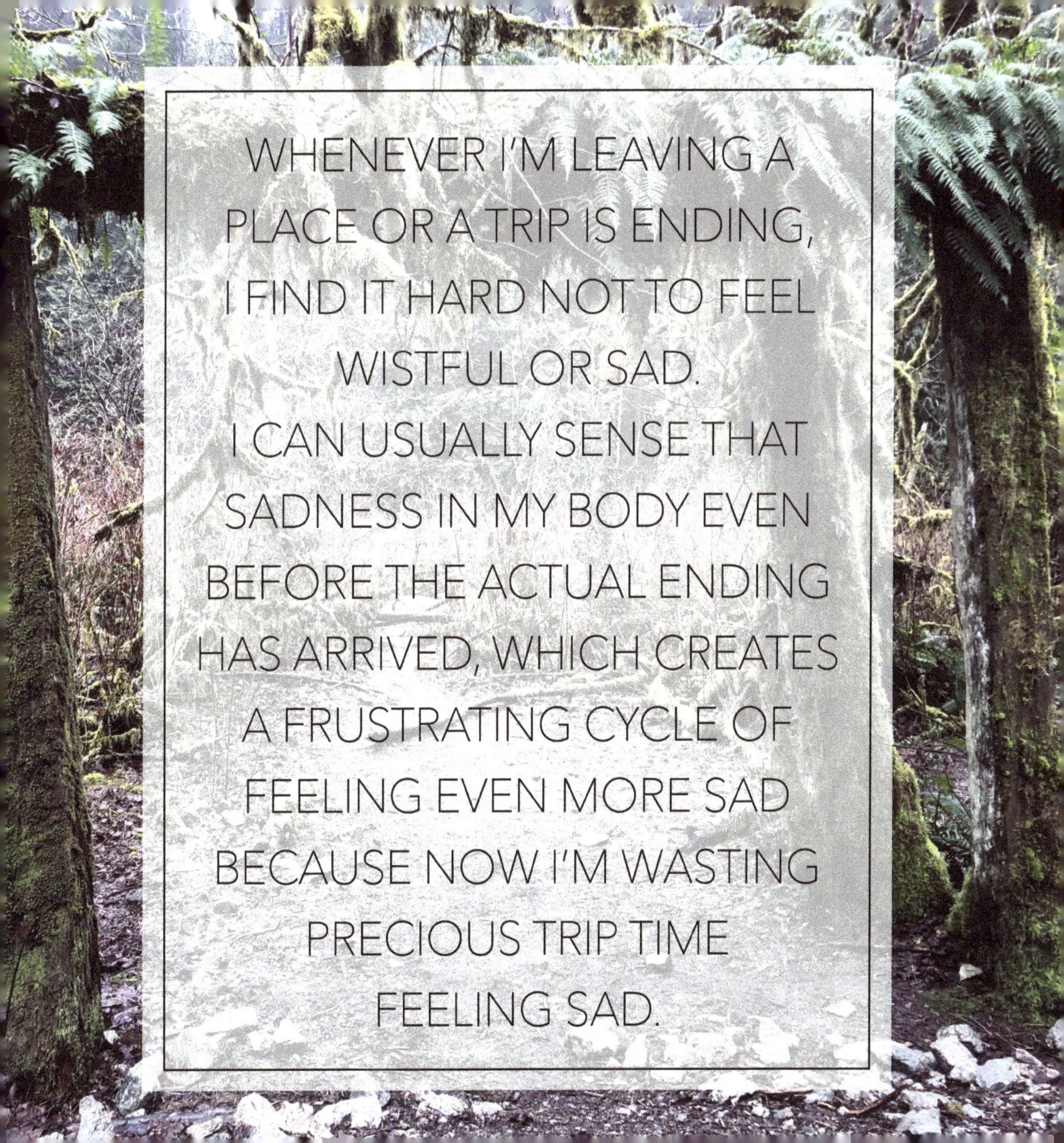

WHENEVER I'M LEAVING A
PLACE OR A TRIP IS ENDING,
I FIND IT HARD NOT TO FEEL
WISTFUL OR SAD.
I CAN USUALLY SENSE THAT
SADNESS IN MY BODY EVEN
BEFORE THE ACTUAL ENDING
HAS ARRIVED, WHICH CREATES
A FRUSTRATING CYCLE OF
FEELING EVEN MORE SAD
BECAUSE NOW I'M WASTING
PRECIOUS TRIP TIME
FEELING SAD.

THERE ARE RULES
FOR WHEN I ALLOW
MYSELF TO HAVE
EMPATHY AND
COMPASSION
AND GRACE
TOWARDS MYSELF.
THESE RULES ARE
COMPLETELY
AND UTTERLY ARBITRARY
(AND CONVOLUTED).

I AM A GIVER.
I WAS RAISED THAT THIS WAS
THE WAY TO BE AND IT BRINGS
ME JOY TO OFFER TO OTHERS.
HOWEVER, WITHIN THIS
NARRATIVE THE ANTAGONIST
TO GIVING IS TAKING.
RECEIVING HAS NO PLACE HERE.
UNTIL THE DAY A DEAR FRIEND
POINTED OUT TO ME THAT
RECEIVING IS THE GREATEST GIFT
I COULD GIVE TO ANOTHER
GIVER.

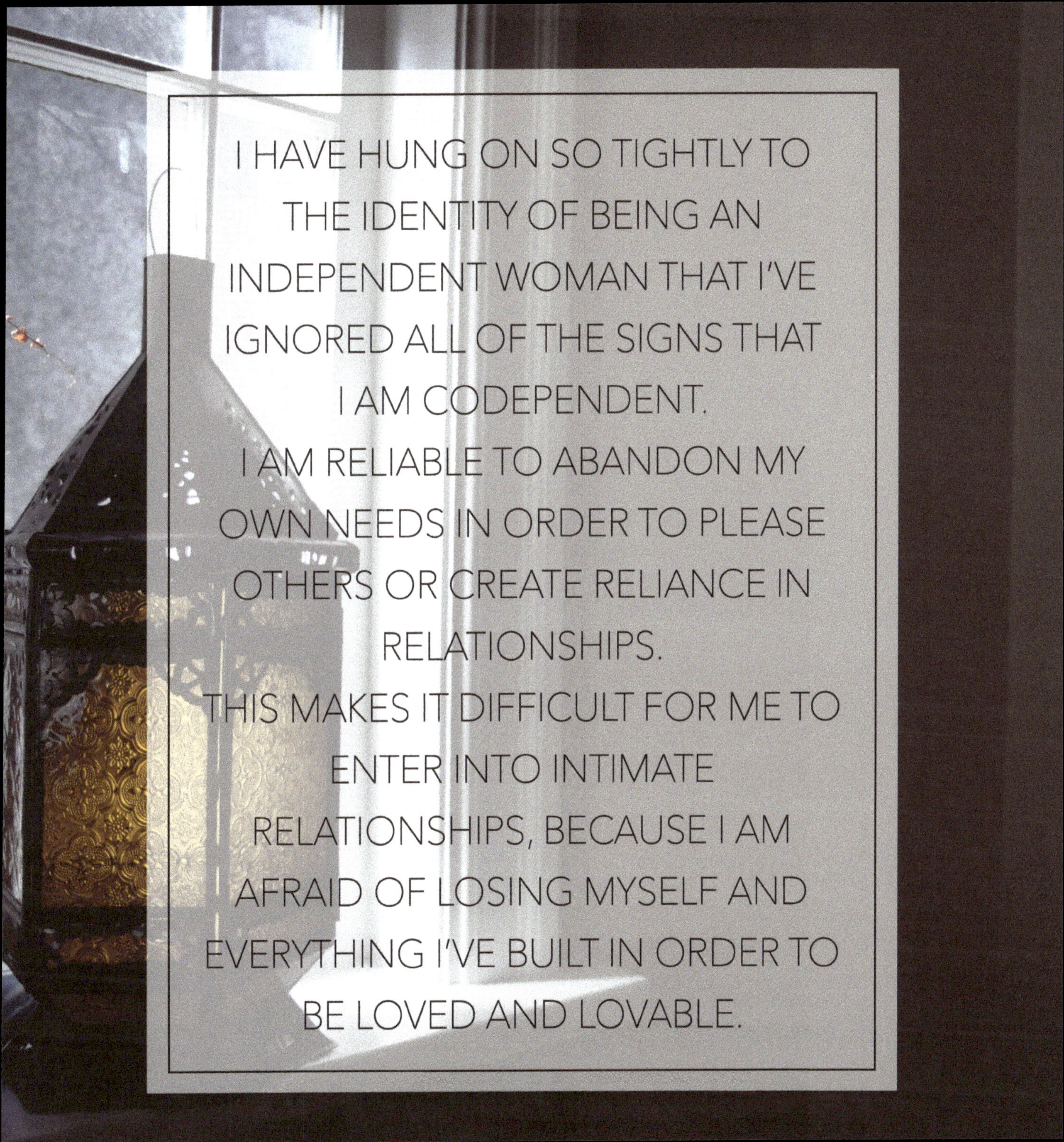

I HAVE HUNG ON SO TIGHTLY TO
THE IDENTITY OF BEING AN
INDEPENDENT WOMAN THAT I'VE
IGNORED ALL OF THE SIGNS THAT
I AM CODEPENDENT.
I AM RELIABLE TO ABANDON MY
OWN NEEDS IN ORDER TO PLEASE
OTHERS OR CREATE RELIANCE IN
RELATIONSHIPS.
THIS MAKES IT DIFFICULT FOR ME TO
ENTER INTO INTIMATE
RELATIONSHIPS, BECAUSE I AM
AFRAID OF LOSING MYSELF AND
EVERYTHING I'VE BUILT IN ORDER TO
BE LOVED AND LOVABLE.

WHEN I WAKE UP WITH AN
EMOTIONAL HANGOVER,
GENERALLY ALL I WANT TO
DO IS STAY HOME ALONE
AND ESCAPE FROM
THE WORLD.
AND GENERALLY
WHAT I NEED TO DO
TO GET BACK TO MYSELF
IS CONNECT WITH PEOPLE
AND BE OF SERVICE.

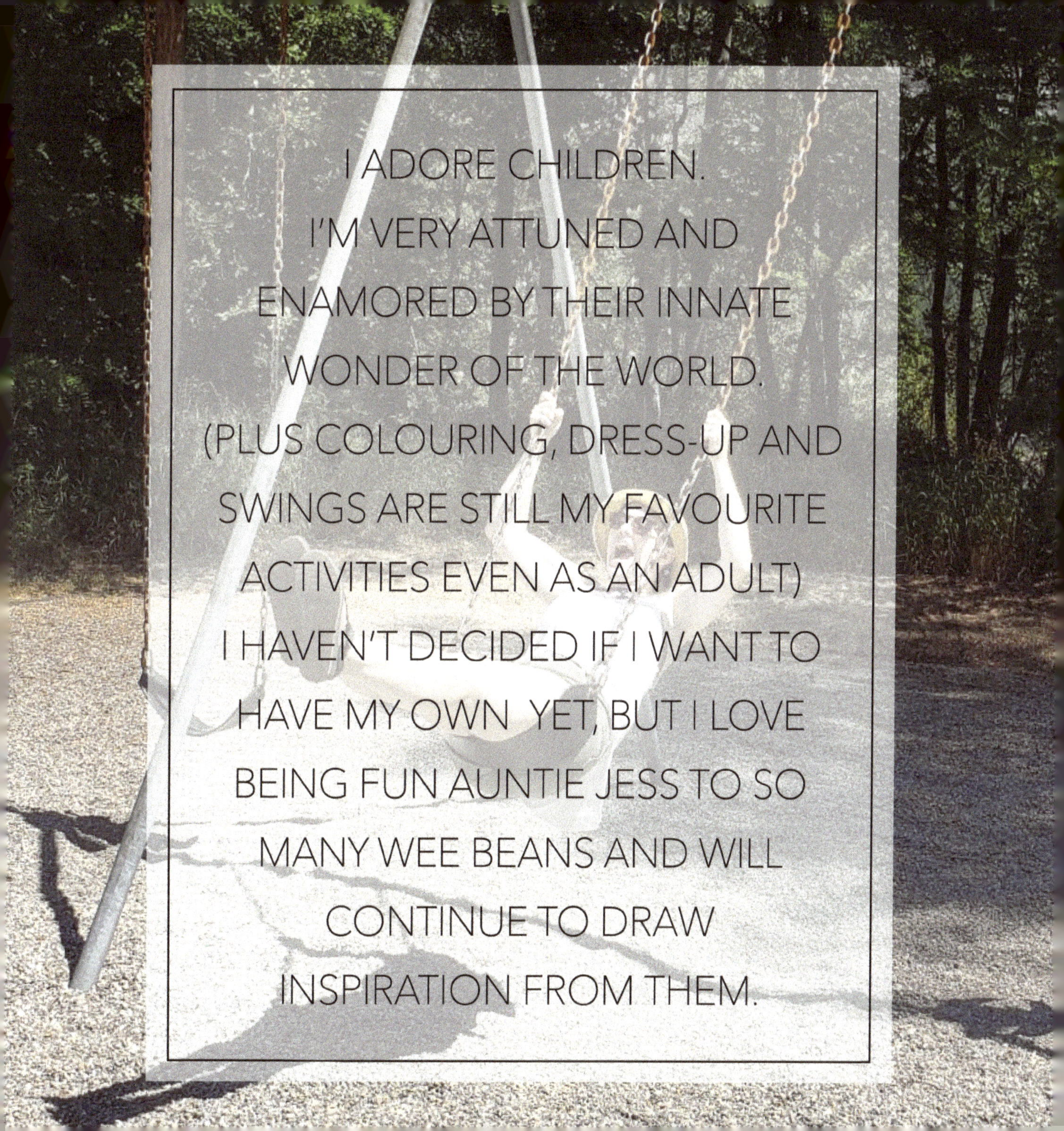

I ADORE CHILDREN.
I'M VERY ATTUNED AND
ENAMORED BY THEIR INNATE
WONDER OF THE WORLD.
(PLUS COLOURING, DRESS-UP AND
SWINGS ARE STILL MY FAVOURITE
ACTIVITIES EVEN AS AN ADULT)
I HAVEN'T DECIDED IF I WANT TO
HAVE MY OWN YET, BUT I LOVE
BEING FUN AUNTIE JESS TO SO
MANY WEE BEANS AND WILL
CONTINUE TO DRAW
INSPIRATION FROM THEM.

I AM BECOMING AWARE THAT I

OFTEN USE NICENESS AND SERVICE

AS A MEANS OF MANIPULATING OTHERS

TO SEE MY VALUE.

THE SUBCONSCIOUS STRATEGY

BEING THAT IF I PERFORM WELL,

I CAN PROVE I AM ENOUGH

USING THE EXTERNAL VALIDATION

AS A METRIC.

THIS DYNAMIC OCCURS

PARTICULARLY OFTEN WITHIN

INTIMATE RELATIONSHIPS.

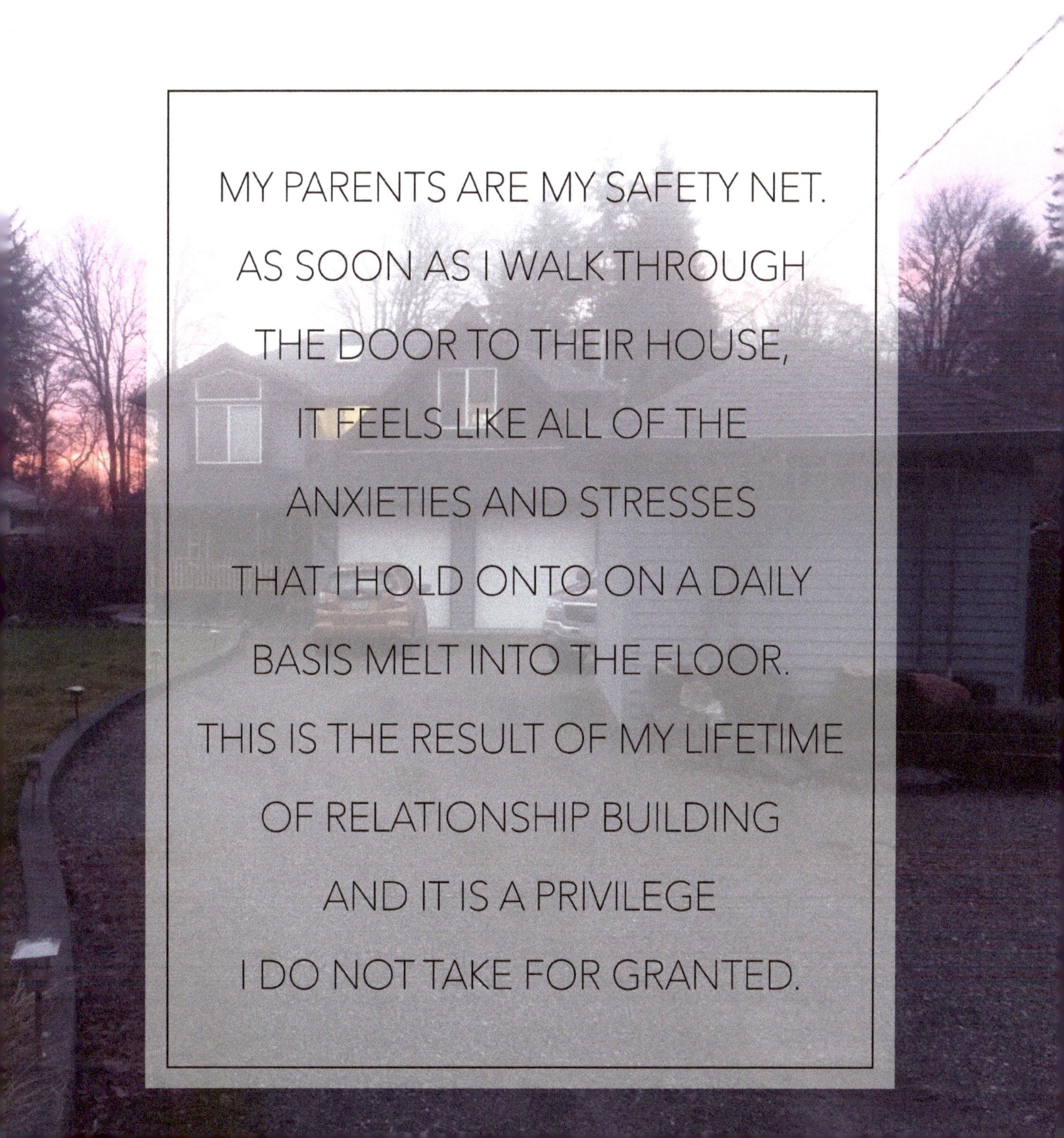

MY PARENTS ARE MY SAFETY NET.

AS SOON AS I WALK THROUGH

THE DOOR TO THEIR HOUSE,

IT FEELS LIKE ALL OF THE

ANXIETIES AND STRESSES

THAT I HOLD ONTO ON A DAILY

BASIS MELT INTO THE FLOOR.

THIS IS THE RESULT OF MY LIFETIME

OF RELATIONSHIP BUILDING

AND IT IS A PRIVILEGE

I DO NOT TAKE FOR GRANTED.

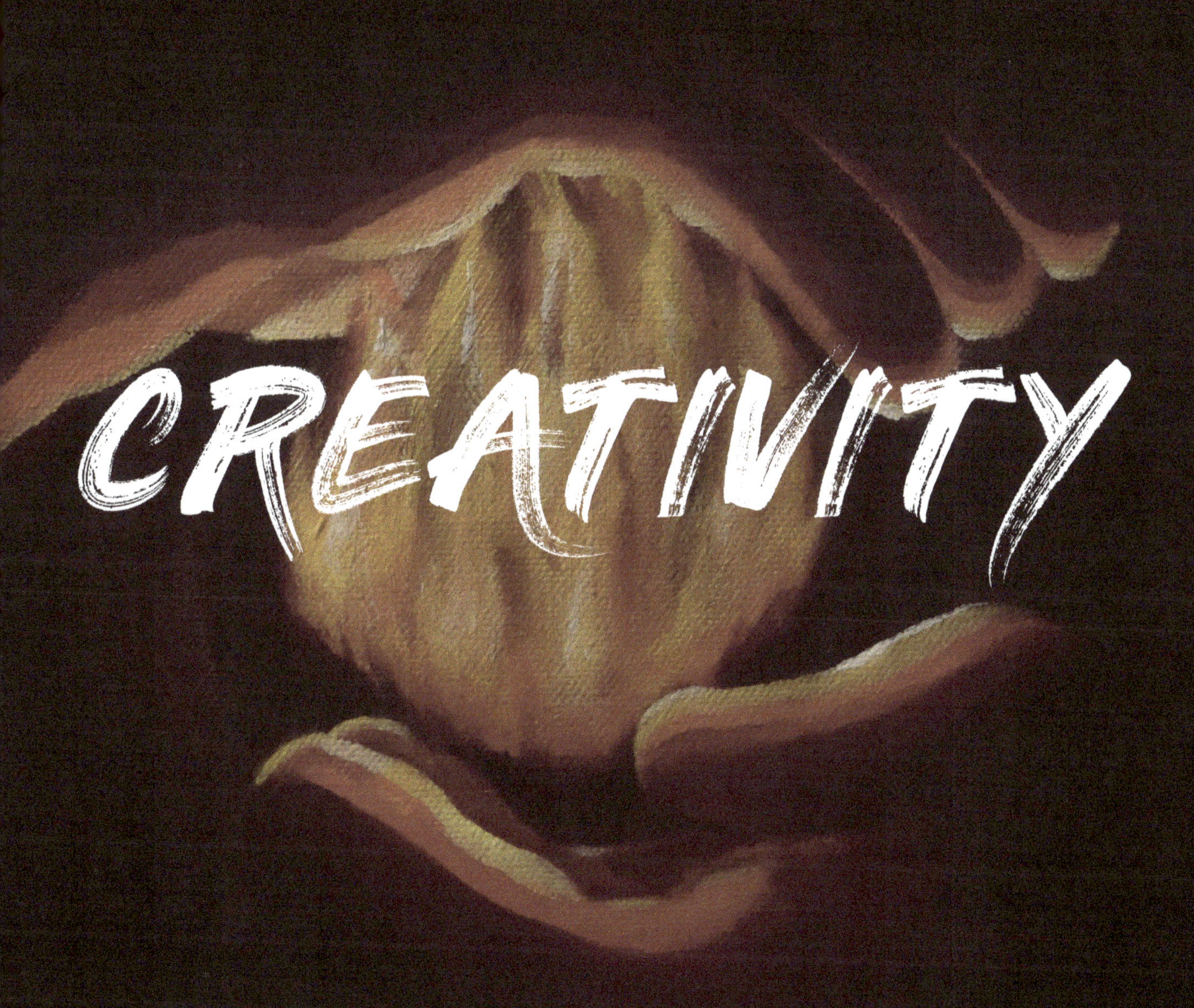
CREATIVITY

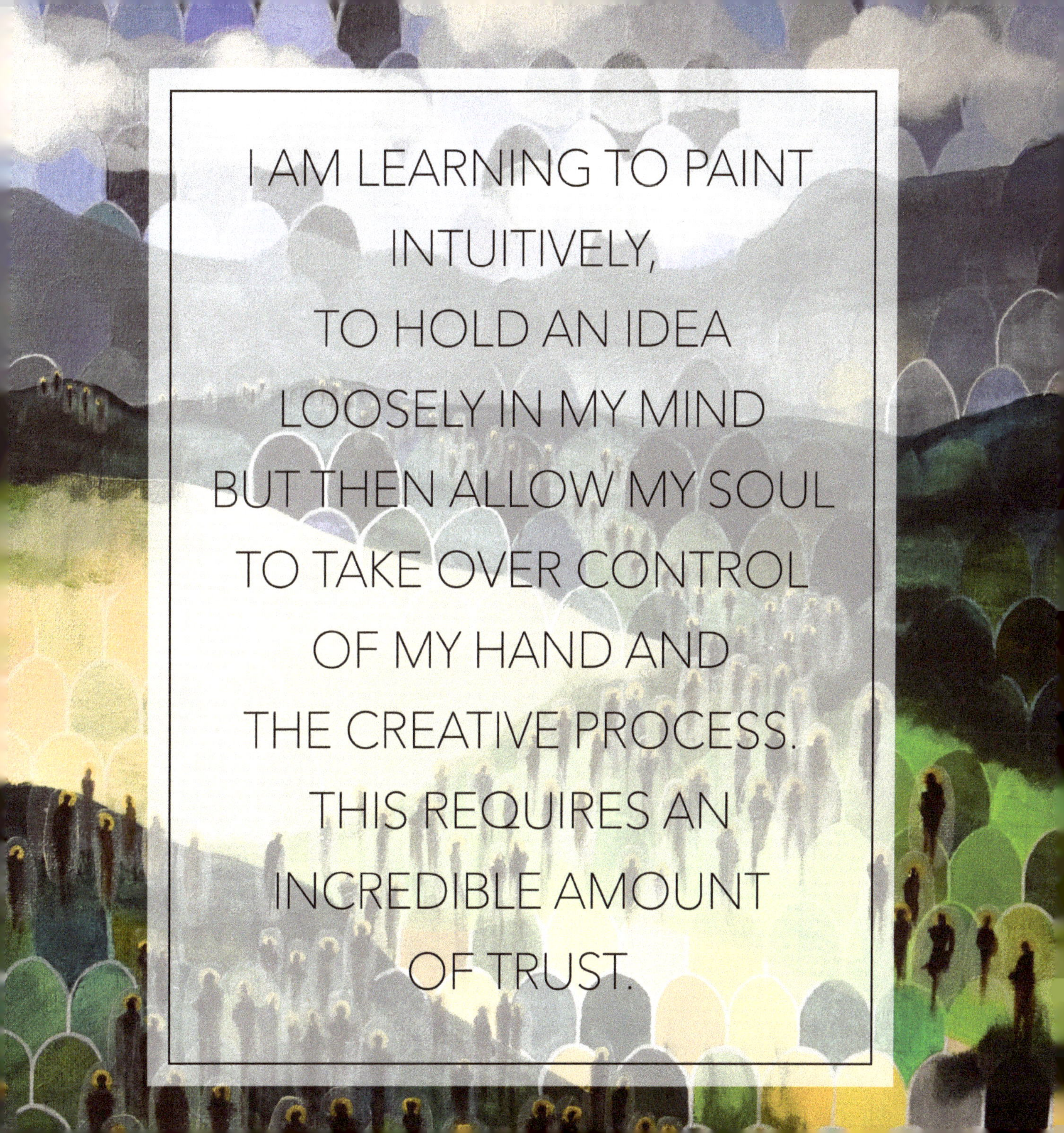
I AM LEARNING TO PAINT
INTUITIVELY,
TO HOLD AN IDEA
LOOSELY IN MY MIND
BUT THEN ALLOW MY SOUL
TO TAKE OVER CONTROL
OF MY HAND AND
THE CREATIVE PROCESS.
THIS REQUIRES AN
INCREDIBLE AMOUNT
OF TRUST.

I SOMETIMES SKETCH OUT
A PAINTING FIRST BEFORE
I PUT BRUSH TO CANVAS.
THIS CALMS MY LOGICAL
BRAIN WITH A PLAN OF
SORTS IN ORDER TO GET
PAST THE ANXIETY OF
STARTING.
EVENTUALLY I NEED TO
PUT THE PLANNING AWAY
THOUGH AND
JUST PAINT.

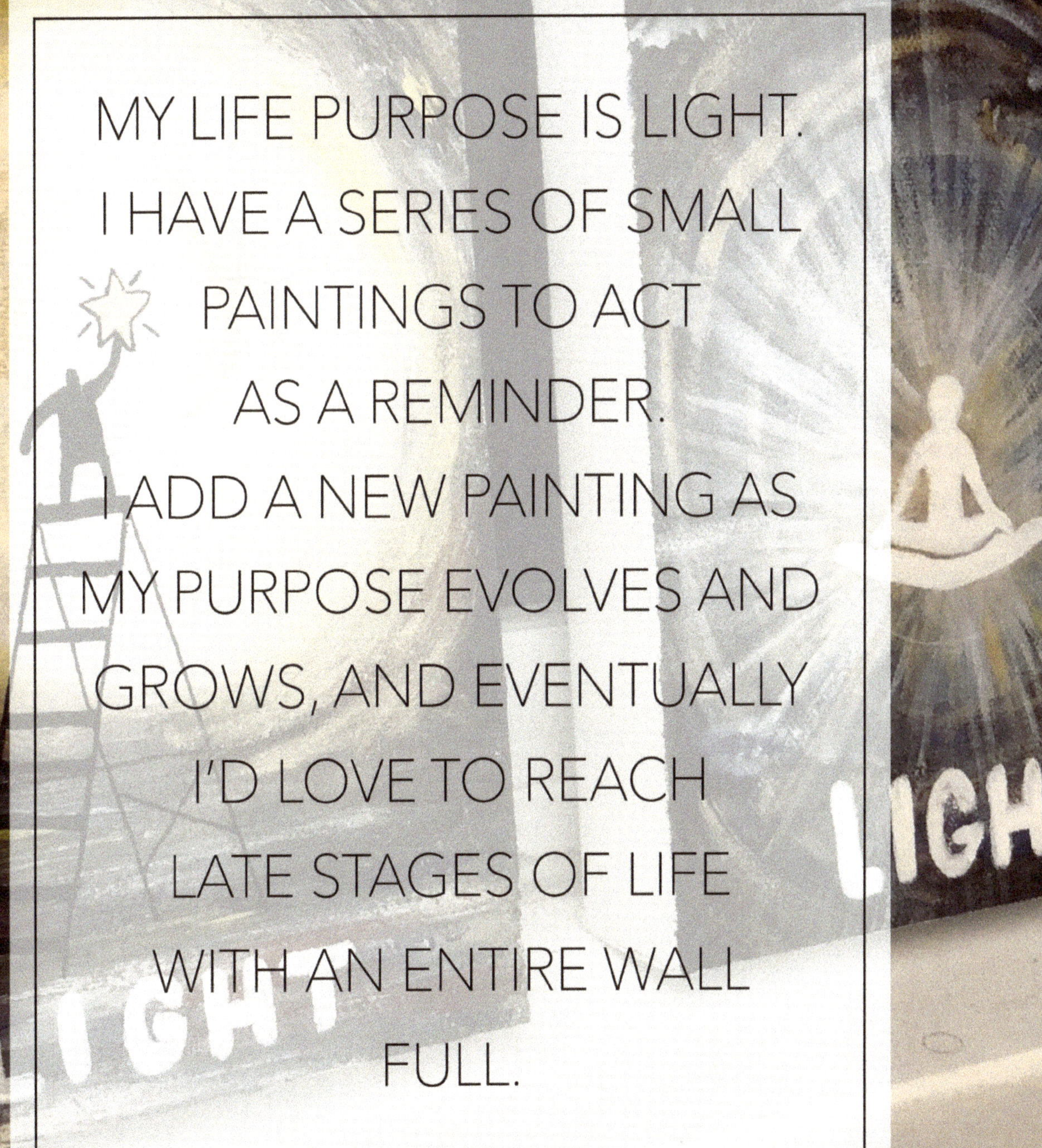

MY LIFE PURPOSE IS LIGHT.
I HAVE A SERIES OF SMALL
PAINTINGS TO ACT
AS A REMINDER.
I ADD A NEW PAINTING AS
MY PURPOSE EVOLVES AND
GROWS, AND EVENTUALLY
I'D LOVE TO REACH
LATE STAGES OF LIFE
WITH AN ENTIRE WALL
FULL.
LIGHT
LIGHT

I'VE NEVER RELATED TO THE SAYING "SUFFER FOR YOUR ART" - AS IF TO CREATE 'GOOD' ART REQUIRES ME TO INTENTIONALLY INVITE HARDSHIP.
CREATIVITY FOR ME IS HEALING, A WAY TO PROCESS MY THOUGHTS AND EXPERIENCES.
HOW ABOUT "DRAW INSPIRATION FROM LIFE AND GROW FOR YOUR ART" INSTEAD?

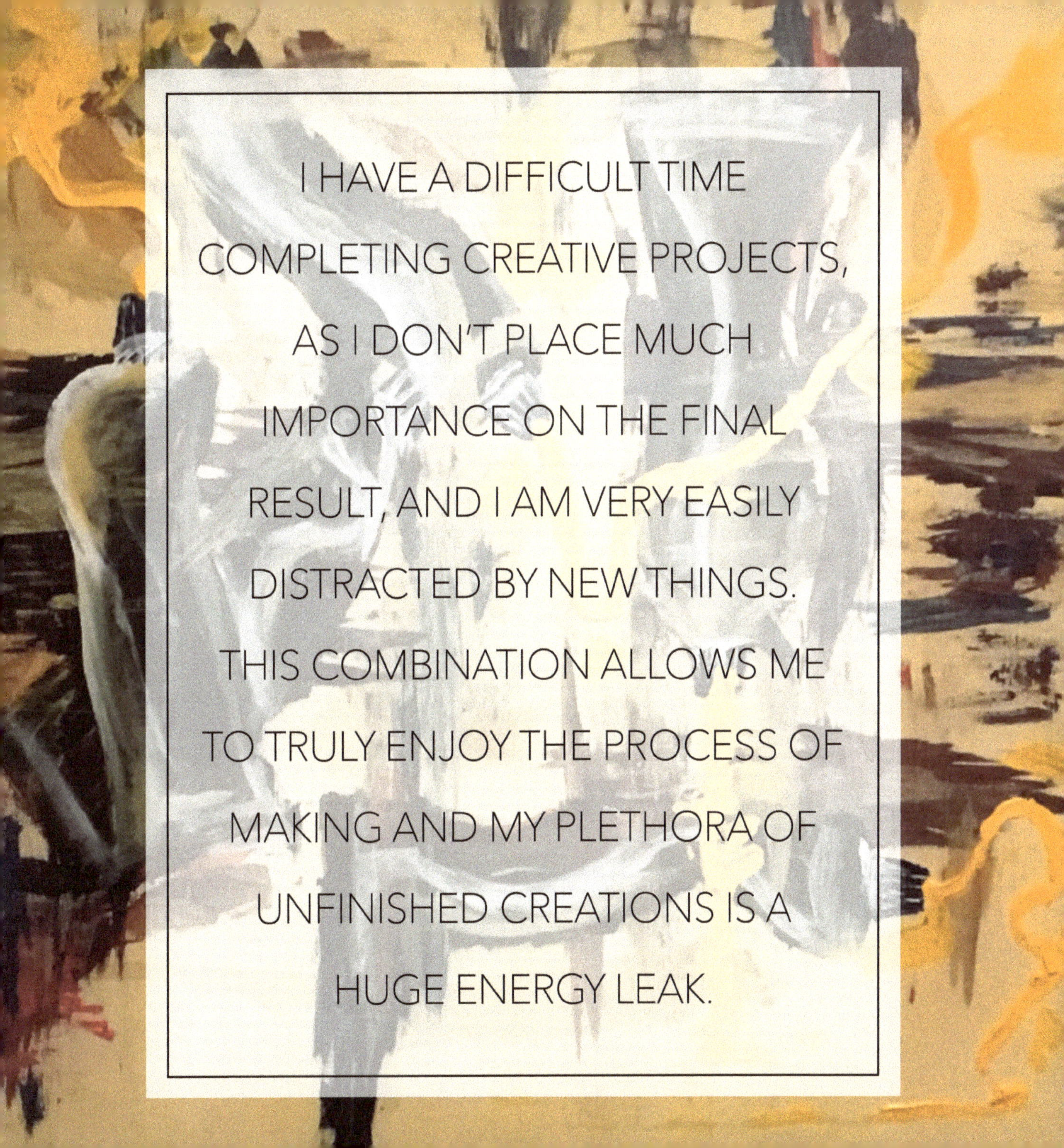

I HAVE A DIFFICULT TIME
COMPLETING CREATIVE PROJECTS,
AS I DON'T PLACE MUCH
IMPORTANCE ON THE FINAL
RESULT, AND I AM VERY EASILY
DISTRACTED BY NEW THINGS.
THIS COMBINATION ALLOWS ME
TO TRULY ENJOY THE PROCESS OF
MAKING AND MY PLETHORA OF
UNFINISHED CREATIONS IS A
HUGE ENERGY LEAK.

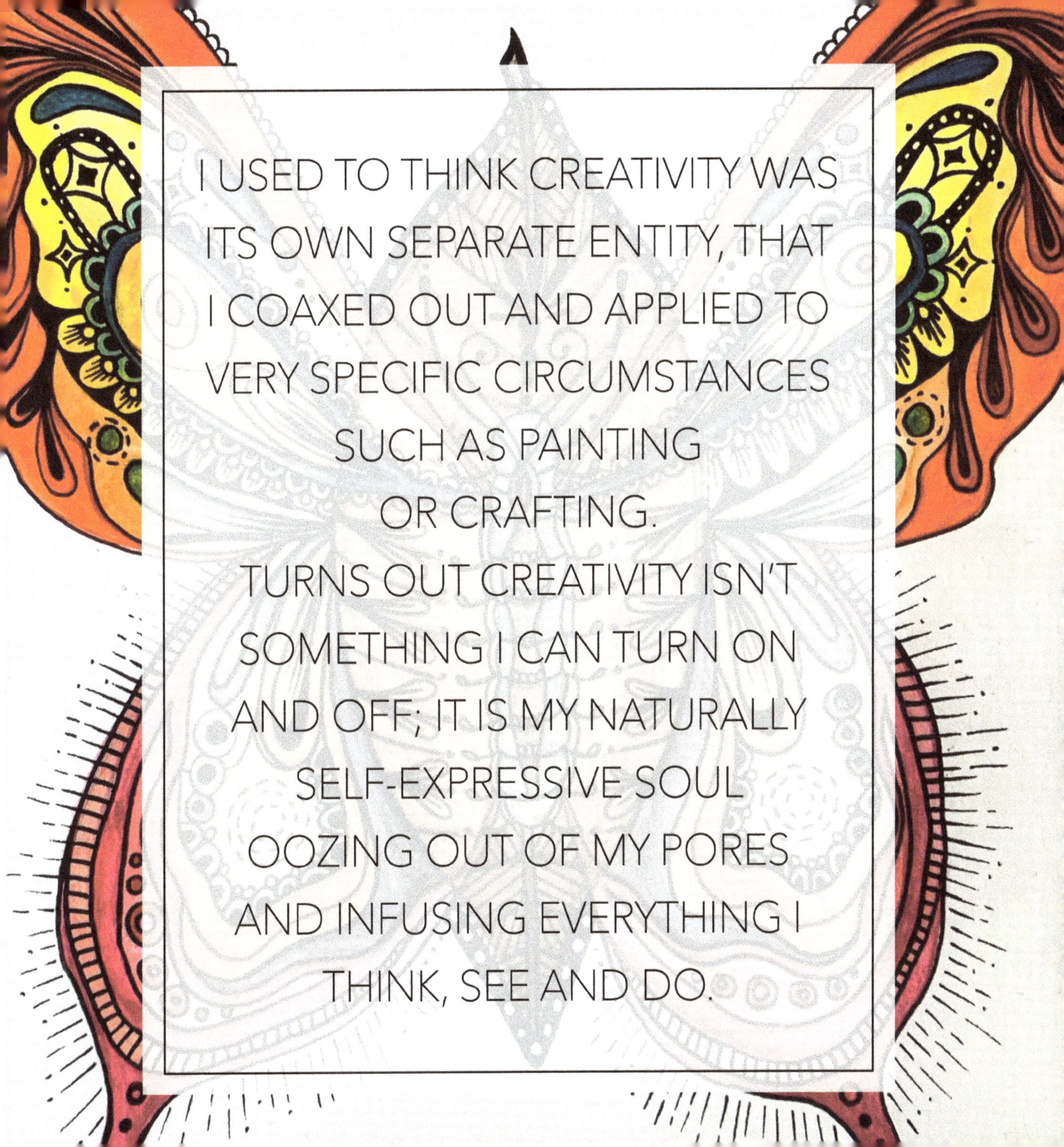

I USED TO THINK CREATIVITY WAS
ITS OWN SEPARATE ENTITY, THAT
I COAXED OUT AND APPLIED TO
VERY SPECIFIC CIRCUMSTANCES
SUCH AS PAINTING
OR CRAFTING.
TURNS OUT CREATIVITY ISN'T
SOMETHING I CAN TURN ON
AND OFF; IT IS MY NATURALLY
SELF-EXPRESSIVE SOUL
OOZING OUT OF MY PORES
AND INFUSING EVERYTHING I
THINK, SEE AND DO.

NOW THAT I'M NOT CAUGHT UP IN AN INTERNAL DEBATE OF WHETHER OR NOT I'M AN ARTIST AND WHETHER OR NOT MY ART IS "GOOD", I CAN FOCUS INSTEAD ON THINGS LIKE THE IMPACT I WANT TO MAKE WITH MY ART.

WHENEVER I NOTICE MYSELF TAKING A LONG TIME TO COMPLETE A PROJECT (AKA I'M AGONIZING OVER WHETHER SOMETHING IS "GOOD ENOUGH"), I TRY AND REMIND MYSELF THAT 100% IS A VERY SUBJECTIVE METRIC. WHEN I LINGER TOO LONG IN THE LIMBO OF "GETTING IT PERFECT," I'M MISSING OUT ON OPPORTUNITIES TO SHARE MY GIFTS, GET FEEDBACK AND GROW. THE EXTRA TIME SPENT TWEAKING IS USUALLY JUST MY FEAR DRIVING.

I AM NOT RESPONSIBLE FOR
CURATING SOMEONE'S
EXPERIENCE OF MY ART.
I HAVE MY OWN EXPERIENCES
CREATING IT AND THEMES THAT
INFUSE THE PROCESS, BUT I THINK
ONCE IT'S OUT IN THE WORLD, I AM
NO LONGER THE AUTHORITY ON
WHAT THOUGHTS OR FEELINGS
IT IS MEANT TO EVOKE.
IF ANYTHING, I THINK THAT
EXPLAINING WHAT MY ART IS ABOUT
TAKES AWAY FROM
THE OPPORTUNITY FOR
A GENUINE REACTION.

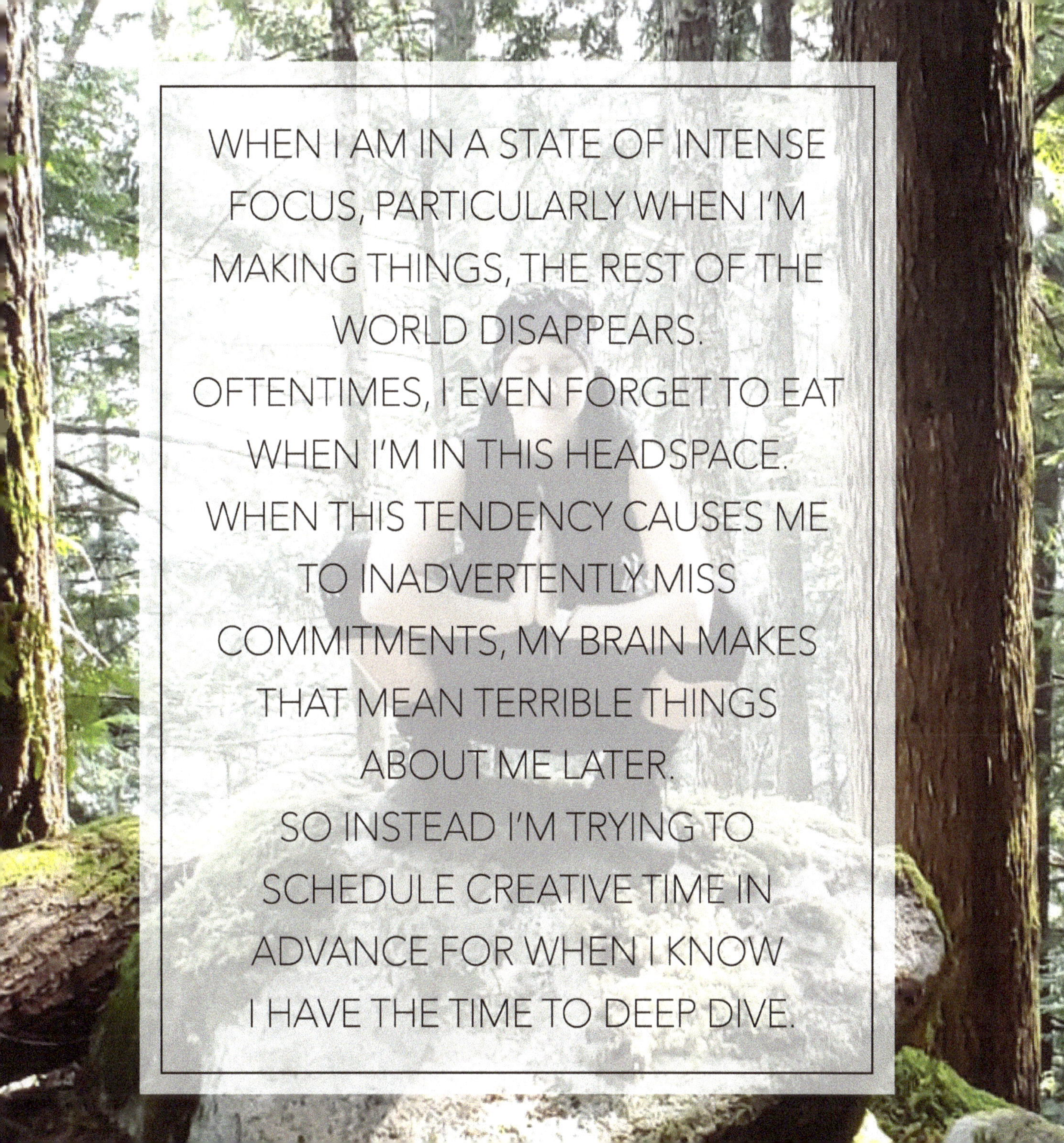

WHEN I AM IN A STATE OF INTENSE
FOCUS, PARTICULARLY WHEN I'M
MAKING THINGS, THE REST OF THE
WORLD DISAPPEARS.
OFTENTIMES, I EVEN FORGET TO EAT
WHEN I'M IN THIS HEADSPACE.
WHEN THIS TENDENCY CAUSES ME
TO INADVERTENTLY MISS
COMMITMENTS, MY BRAIN MAKES
THAT MEAN TERRIBLE THINGS
ABOUT ME LATER.
SO INSTEAD I'M TRYING TO
SCHEDULE CREATIVE TIME IN
ADVANCE FOR WHEN I KNOW
I HAVE THE TIME TO DEEP DIVE.

I'VE COME TO REALIZE THAT HAVING MORE TIME DOES NOT EQUAL SUCCESS IN CREATIVE ENDEAVOURS IF I HAVEN'T DONE THE WORK BEFOREHAND TO PROCESS AND GET AHEAD OF THE BULLSHIT MY EGO MAKES UP TO KEEP ME STUCK AND PLAYING SMALL.
"HAVING NO TIME" IS A CONVENIENT SURFACE LAYER EXCUSE.
MY BULLSHIT IS MY EGO'S LAST LINE OF DEFENSE.

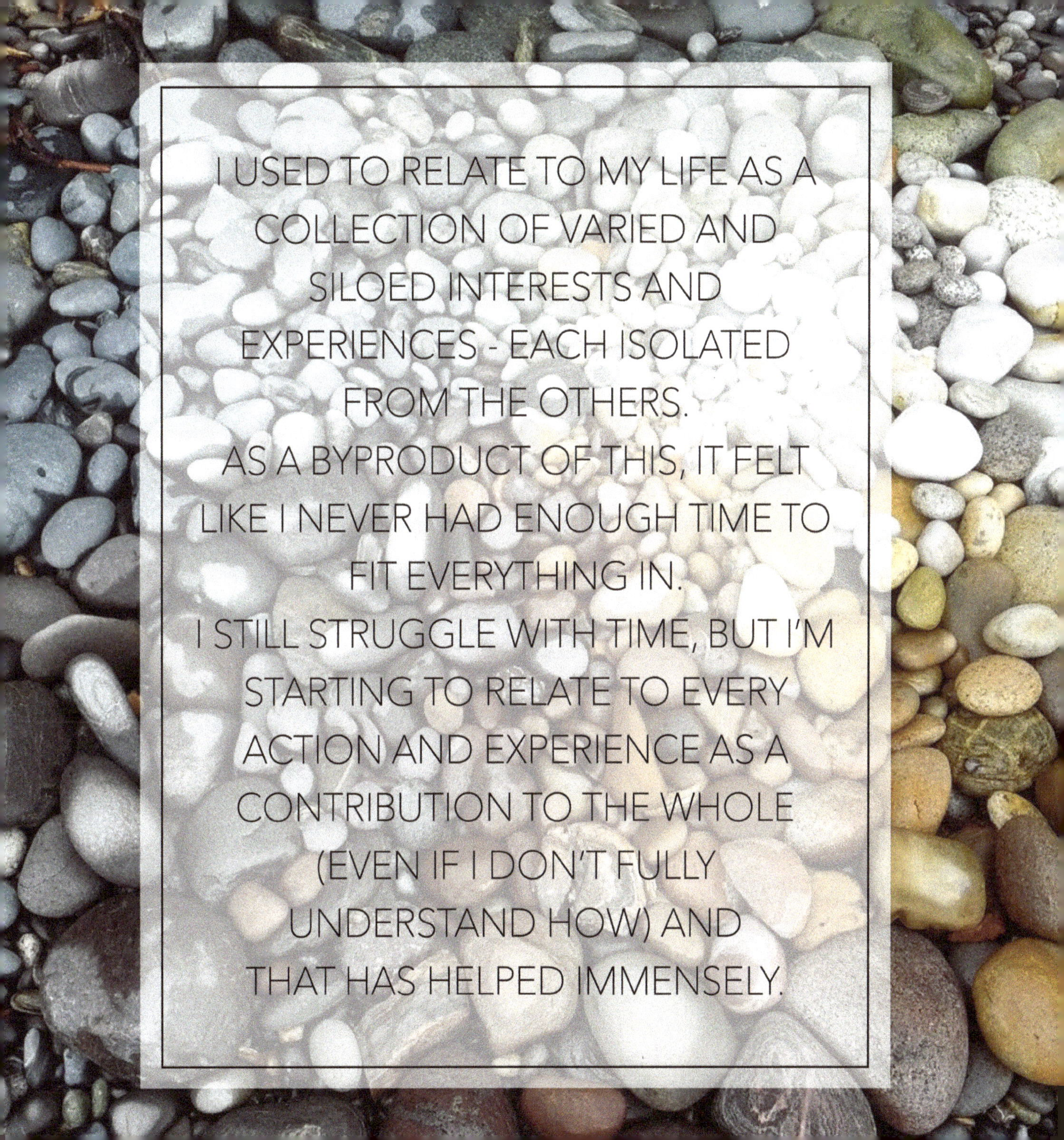
I USED TO RELATE TO MY LIFE AS A
COLLECTION OF VARIED AND
SILOED INTERESTS AND
EXPERIENCES - EACH ISOLATED
FROM THE OTHERS.
AS A BYPRODUCT OF THIS, IT FELT
LIKE I NEVER HAD ENOUGH TIME TO
FIT EVERYTHING IN.
I STILL STRUGGLE WITH TIME, BUT I'M
STARTING TO RELATE TO EVERY
ACTION AND EXPERIENCE AS A
CONTRIBUTION TO THE WHOLE
(EVEN IF I DON'T FULLY
UNDERSTAND HOW) AND
THAT HAS HELPED IMMENSELY.

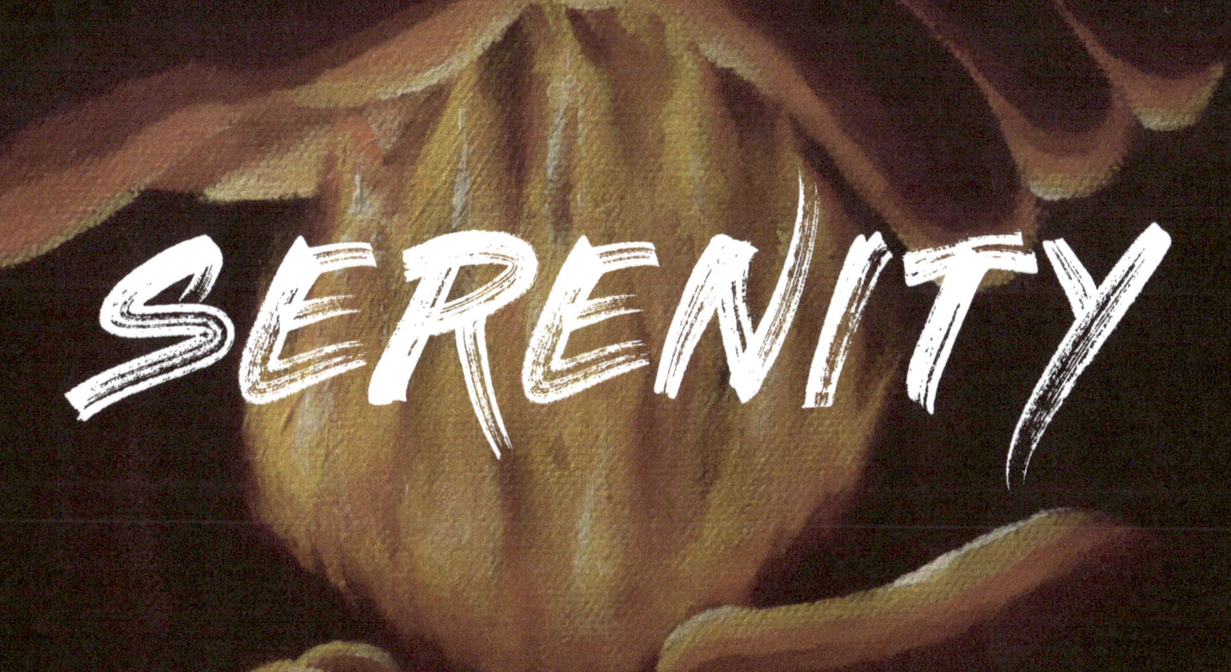
SERENITY

I AM LISTENING TO MY BODY
AND INNER VOICE FOR
GUIDANCE ON WHAT I NEED
MOMENT TO MOMENT.
THIS IS FLYING IN THE FACE OF
MY SELF-SABOTAGE
TENDENCIES, THAT
GENERALLY LEAVE ME
FEELING SIMULTANEOUSLY
MAD AT MYSELF FOR NOT
DOING ENOUGH AND NOT
RESTING ENOUGH

WHENEVER I'M FEELING UNTETHERED IN ANY WAY, IT IS USUALLY AN INDICATION FOR ME TO PUT EXTRA ATTENTION ON MY WELLBEING PRACTICES.
BACK TO THE BASICS:
- SLEEP

- DRINK WATER

- EXERCISE

- EAT GOOD FOOD
(NOT NECESSARILY
IN THAT ORDER)

SOLO
ADVENTURING
IN NATURE
IS THE BEST WAY
I'VE FOUND TO
COMMUNE WITH
[GOD/UNIVERSE/
SPIRIT/THE GREAT
UNKNOWN].

NOTHING IS COMING
TO ME TO WRITE
TODAY
SO RATHER THAN
FORCE IT,
I'M GOING TO TAKE IT
AS A SIGN THAT
NOTHING
IS WHAT IS NEEDED.

I'VE BEEN LEARNING HOW TO TRUST THE UNIVERSE, AND I AM INDEED MORE TRUSTING OVERALL AS A RESULT. HOWEVER I ALSO INADVERTENTLY SET UP MY SPIRITUAL SURRENDER IN SUCH A WAY THAT IF THE EXACT RESULTS I WANT DON'T MANIFEST, I MAKE IT MEAN I'M UNWORTHY.
THE UNIVERSE MUST NOT LOVE ME ENOUGH TO DELIVER ON MY REQUEST. USUALLY WHEN THIS MINDSET APPEARS, IT'S IN CONJUNCTION WITH ME BEING OUT OF THE FLOW OF ACTION AND WAITING FOR SOMETHING TO HAPPEN. THE NEW GOAL IS TO PUT RUBBER TO THE ROAD AND MEET THE UNIVERSE HALF WAY.

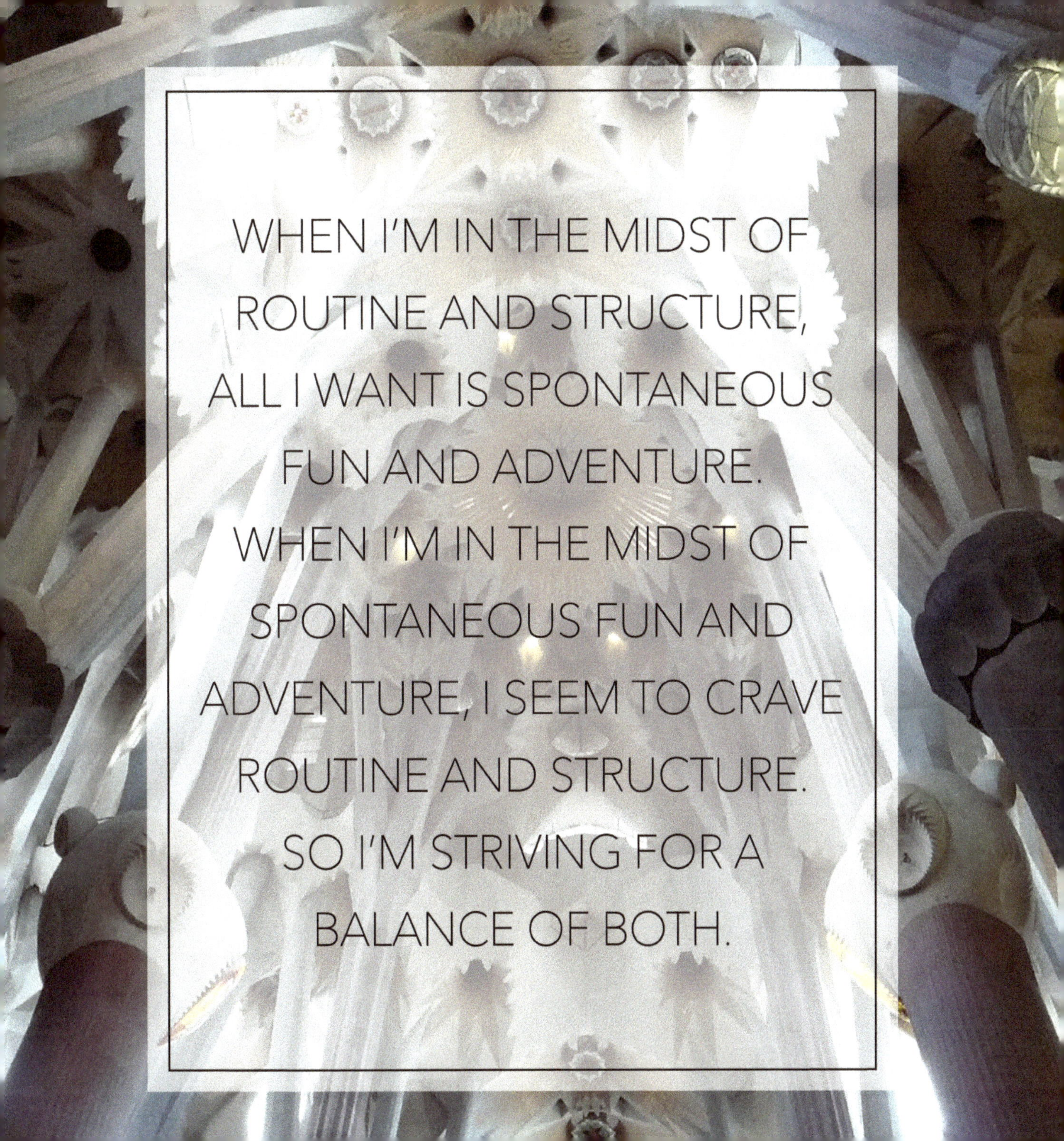

WHEN I'M IN THE MIDST OF
ROUTINE AND STRUCTURE,
ALL I WANT IS SPONTANEOUS
FUN AND ADVENTURE.
WHEN I'M IN THE MIDST OF
SPONTANEOUS FUN AND
ADVENTURE, I SEEM TO CRAVE
ROUTINE AND STRUCTURE.
SO I'M STRIVING FOR A
BALANCE OF BOTH.

INFLOW MINUS OUTFLOW
EQUALS WHAT'S SO.
I USED TO THINK THIS
EQUATION ONLY
APPLIED TO MONEY
AND BUDGETTING,
BUT I'M QUICKLY
REALIZING IT APPLIES
JUST AS MUCH
TO MY ENERGY.

I AVOID FEELING BORED OR
"BEING BORING"
BECAUSE I EQUATE IT WITH
BEING LAZY OR UNPRODUCTIVE.
I "SHOULD" BE BUSY ALL THE
TIME, THEREFORE I ALSO HAVE
A HARD TIME INTENTIONALLY
ALLOWING SPACE FOR REST.
MY NERVOUS SYSTEM IS
ALWAYS THANKFUL FOR
SOME BOREDOM.

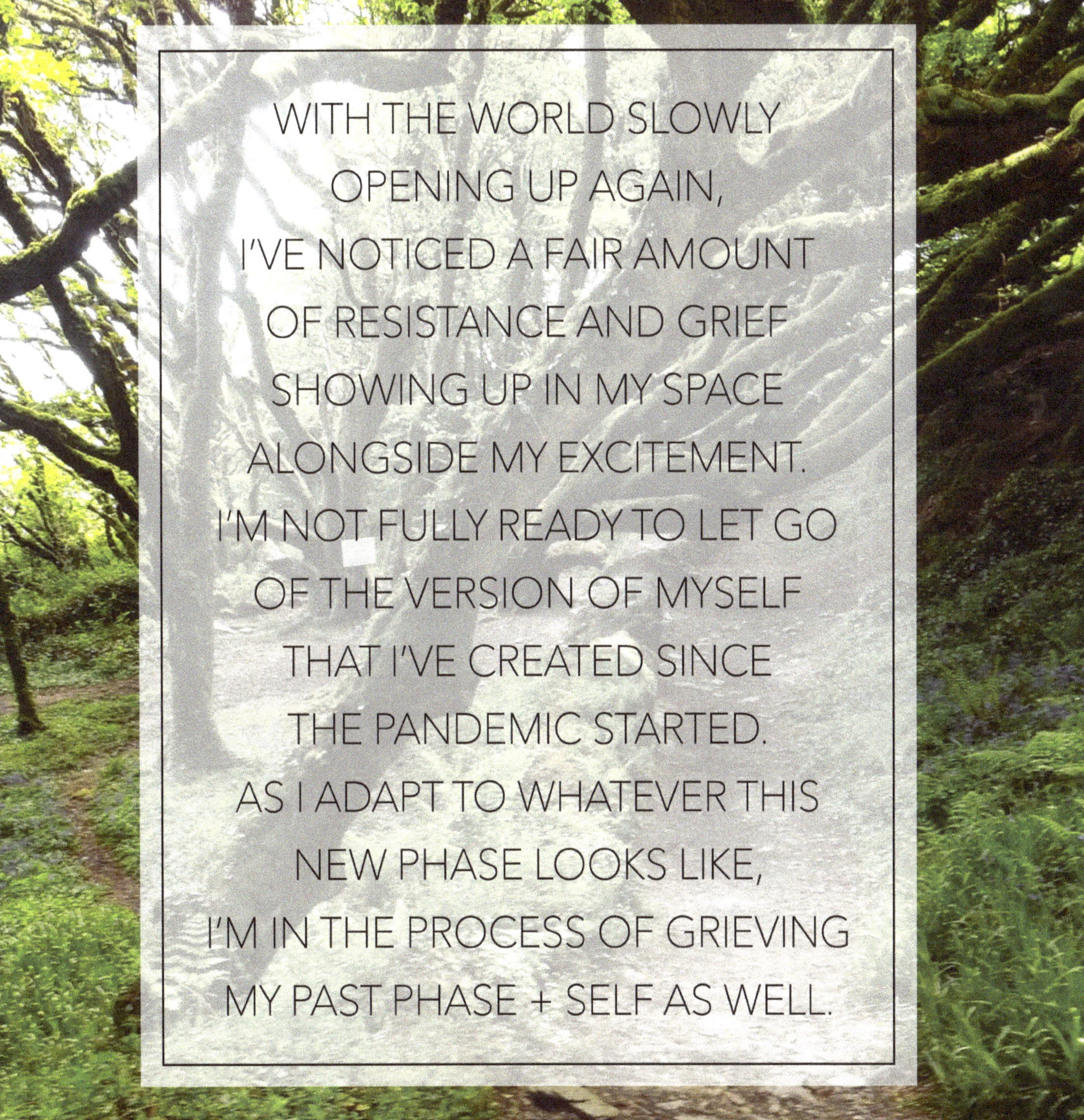

WITH THE WORLD SLOWLY
OPENING UP AGAIN,
I'VE NOTICED A FAIR AMOUNT
OF RESISTANCE AND GRIEF
SHOWING UP IN MY SPACE
ALONGSIDE MY EXCITEMENT.
I'M NOT FULLY READY TO LET GO
OF THE VERSION OF MYSELF
THAT I'VE CREATED SINCE
THE PANDEMIC STARTED.
AS I ADAPT TO WHATEVER THIS
NEW PHASE LOOKS LIKE,
I'M IN THE PROCESS OF GRIEVING
MY PAST PHASE + SELF AS WELL.

I AM THE QUEEN OF
OVERCOMPLICATION.
IF THERE'S A HARDEST WAY
TO ACCOMPLISH A TASK,
I PROBABLY TRIED THAT FIRST.
NOT ON PURPOSE - I GENERALLY DON'T
REALIZE IT'S THE HARD WAY UNTIL
SOMEONE ELSE POINTS OUT
A SIMPLER ALTERNATIVE.
I THINK MY STORY THAT
"MORE WORK = MORE VALUE"
HAS BECOME SO INGRAINED OVER TIME,
THAT I PICK THE MORE COMPLICATED
SOLUTION SUBCONSCIOUSLY
TO FIT THAT MINDSET.

I'M BREAKING UP WITH THE
BULLSHIT THAT I'M ALWAYS
"BEHIND" WHERE I THINK
I SHOULD BE.
THIS TENDS TO SPIRAL INTO
VARIOUS FORMS OF
STRATEGY AND SELF SABOTAGE
IN ORDER TO "CATCH UP."
THE TRUTH IS,
I AM EXACTLY WHERE
I'M SUPPOSED TO BE.

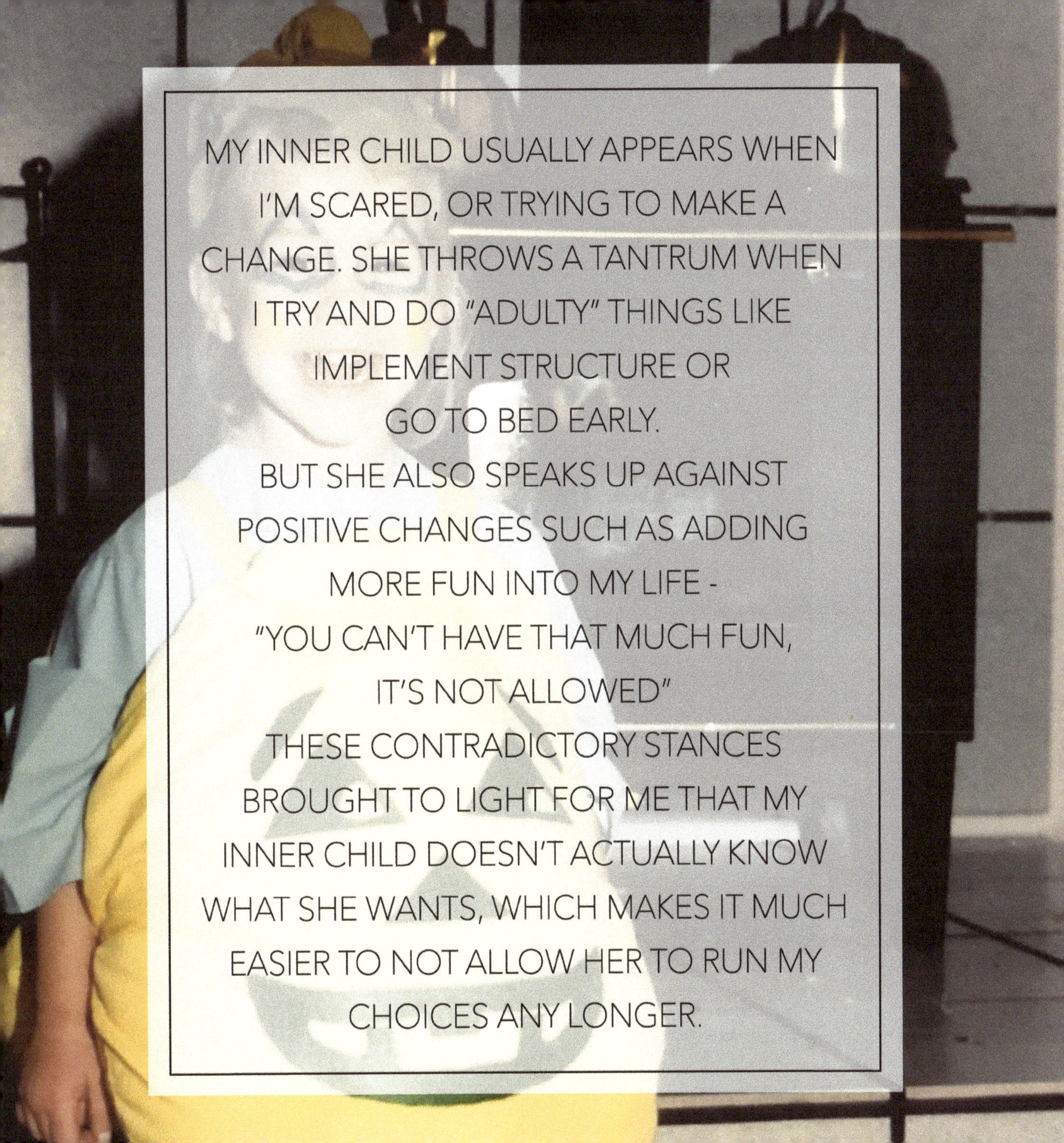
MY INNER CHILD USUALLY APPEARS WHEN
I'M SCARED, OR TRYING TO MAKE A
CHANGE. SHE THROWS A TANTRUM WHEN
I TRY AND DO "ADULTY" THINGS LIKE
IMPLEMENT STRUCTURE OR
GO TO BED EARLY.
BUT SHE ALSO SPEAKS UP AGAINST
POSITIVE CHANGES SUCH AS ADDING
MORE FUN INTO MY LIFE -
"YOU CAN'T HAVE THAT MUCH FUN,
IT'S NOT ALLOWED"
THESE CONTRADICTORY STANCES
BROUGHT TO LIGHT FOR ME THAT MY
INNER CHILD DOESN'T ACTUALLY KNOW
WHAT SHE WANTS, WHICH MAKES IT MUCH
EASIER TO NOT ALLOW HER TO RUN MY
CHOICES ANY LONGER.

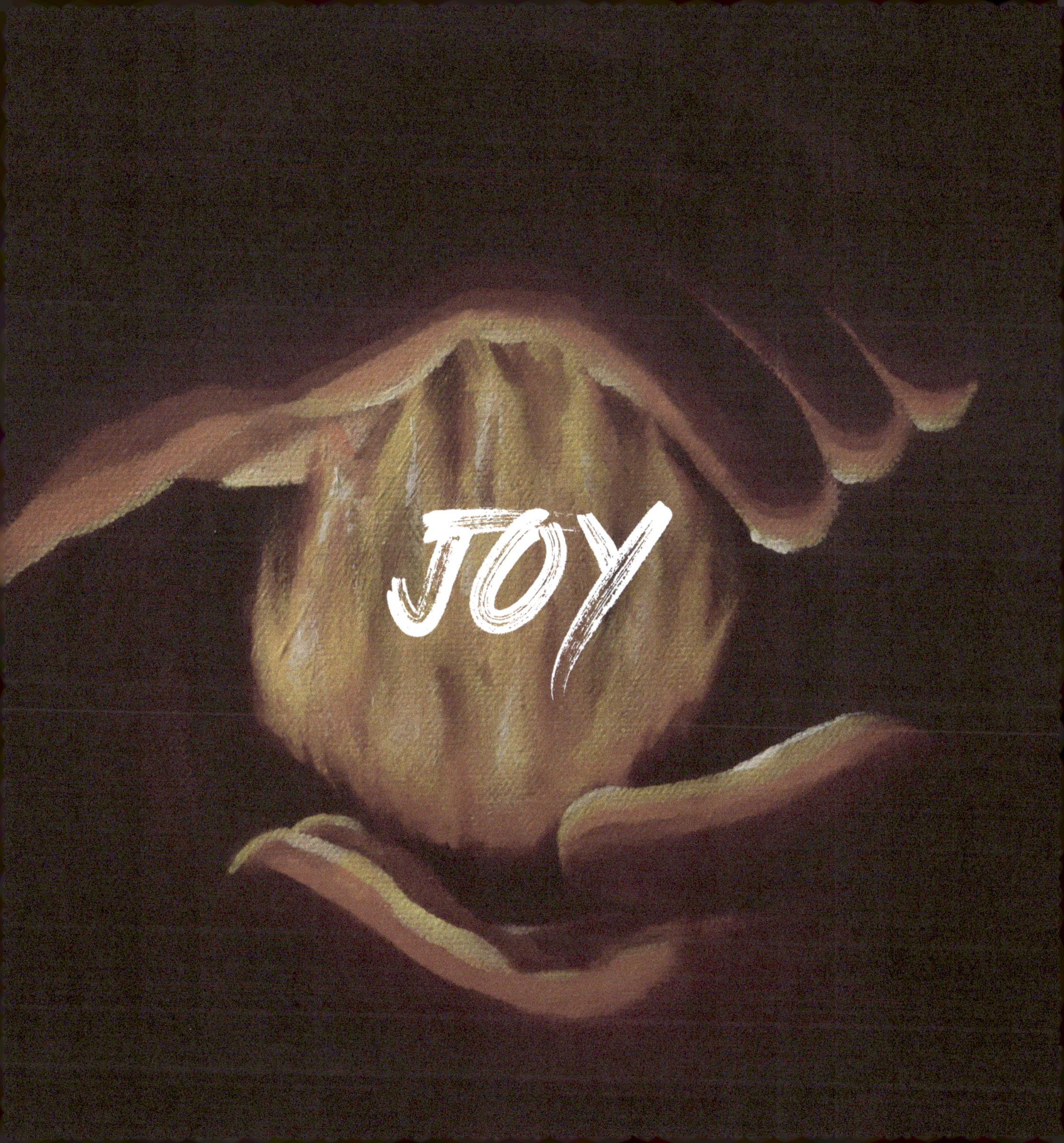
JOY

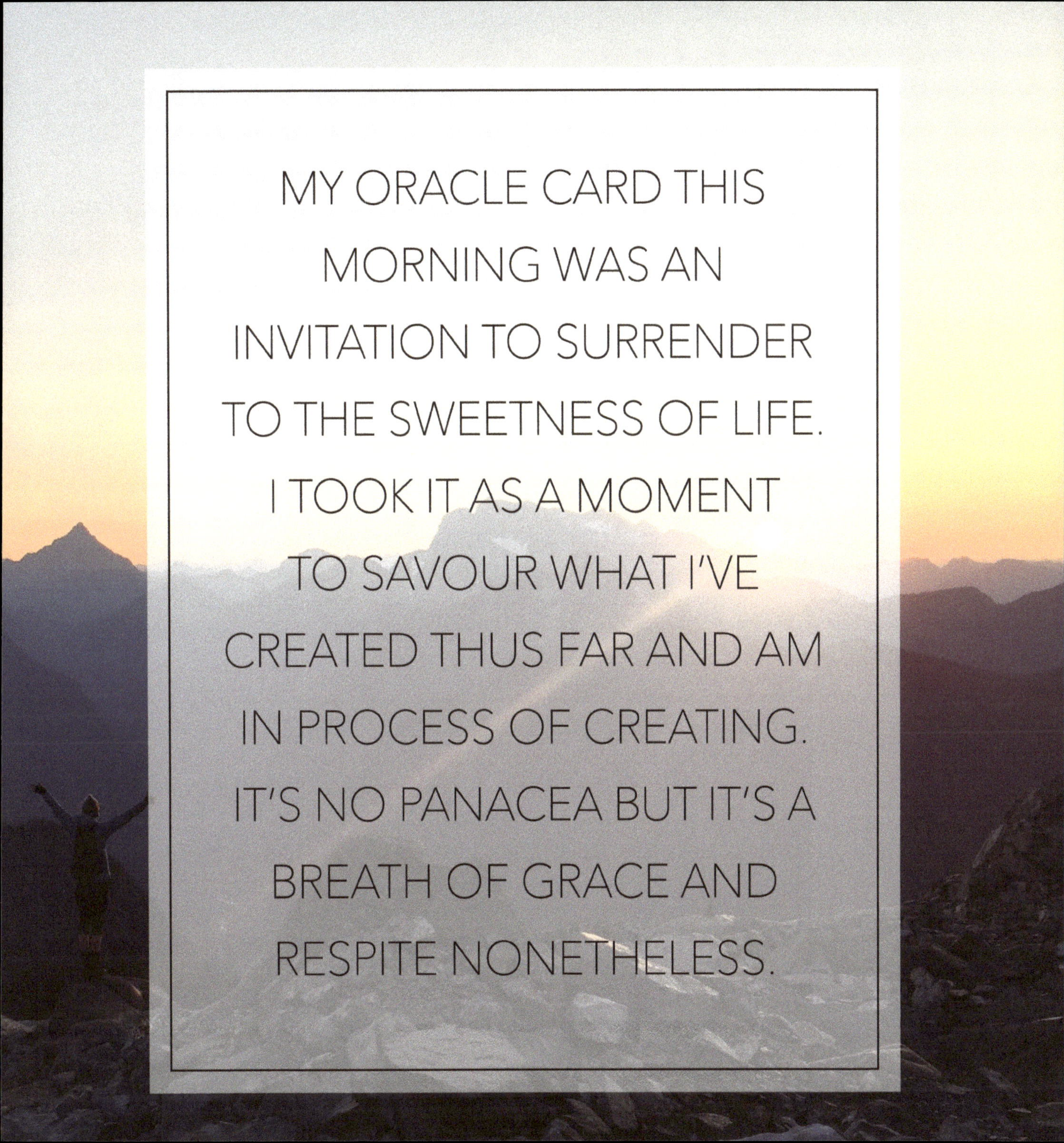

MY ORACLE CARD THIS
MORNING WAS AN
INVITATION TO SURRENDER
TO THE SWEETNESS OF LIFE.
I TOOK IT AS A MOMENT
TO SAVOUR WHAT I'VE
CREATED THUS FAR AND AM
IN PROCESS OF CREATING.
IT'S NO PANACEA BUT IT'S A
BREATH OF GRACE AND
RESPITE NONETHELESS.

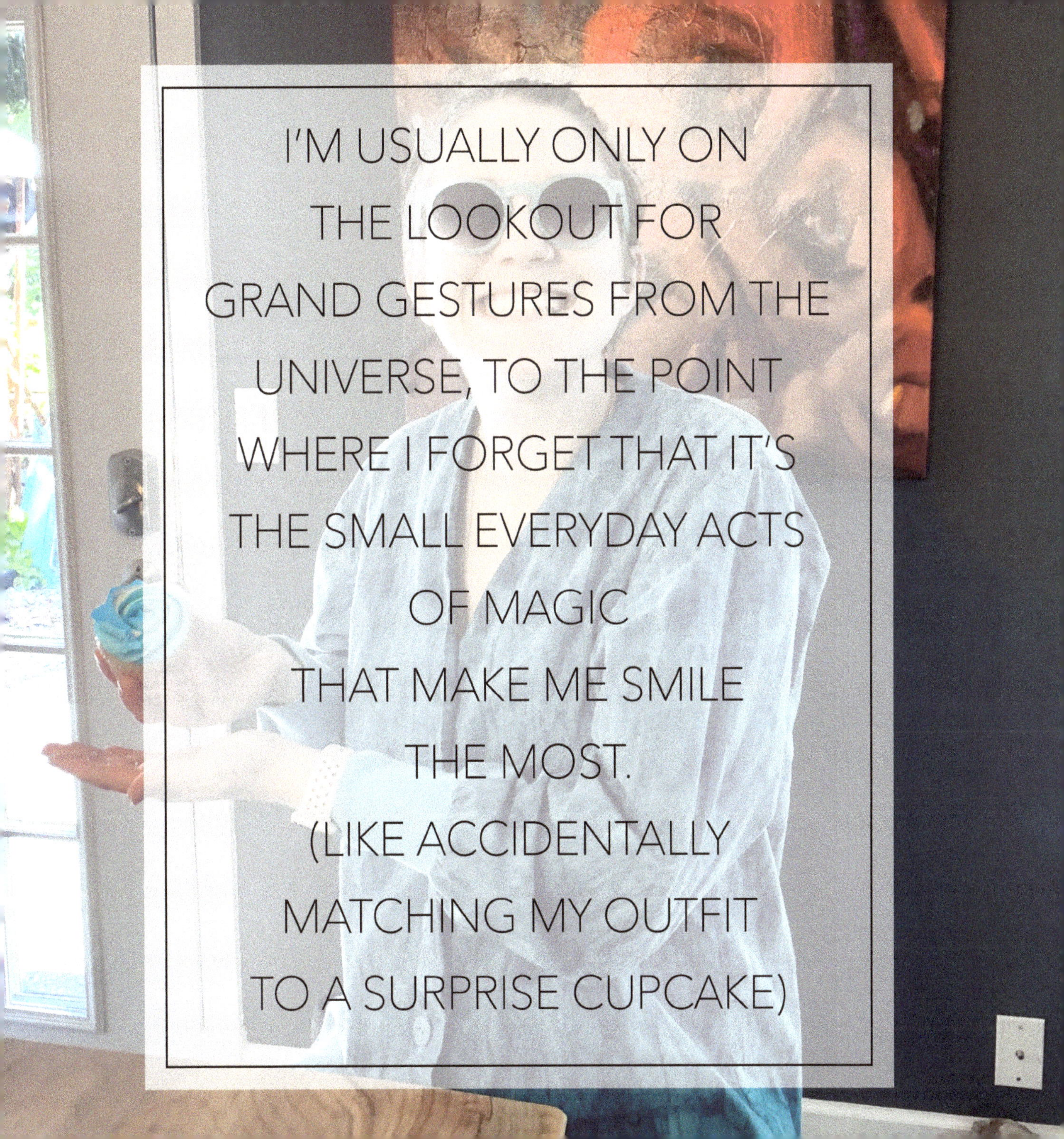

I'M USUALLY ONLY ON
THE LOOKOUT FOR
GRAND GESTURES FROM THE
UNIVERSE, TO THE POINT
WHERE I FORGET THAT IT'S
THE SMALL EVERYDAY ACTS
OF MAGIC
THAT MAKE ME SMILE
THE MOST.
(LIKE ACCIDENTALLY
MATCHING MY OUTFIT
TO A SURPRISE CUPCAKE)

HAVE YOU EVER WANTED
SOMETHING, PUT A REQUEST OUT
INTO THE UNIVERSE, PROMPTLY
FORGOTTEN ALL ABOUT IT, THEN
RECEIVED THAT SOMETHING LATER
FROM A FRIEND IN THE MOST
BEAUTIFULLY ORGANIC WAY
POSSIBLE?
FOR ME, THESE MOMENTS ARE A
WONDERFUL REMINDER THAT
ASKING FOR WHAT I WANT DOESN'T
LESSEN THE IMPACT OF GIFT GIVING -
IT ARGUABLY MAKES IT EVEN MORE
SPECIAL.

I AM AFRAID OF MY ANGER.
BY DEFAULT I LOCK IT AWAY IN
THE DUSTY ATTIC OF MY
HEART SPACE,
AN INVISIBLE INFERNO.
THIS WORKS GREAT UNTIL THE
BUILD UP INEVITABLY BURSTS
OUT AT THE SEAMS.
BECAUSE I'VE SPENT SO LITTLE
TIME GETTING TO KNOW THE
NUANCES OF MY ANGER, I AM
AFRAID OF THE UNKNOWN AND
THE CYCLE OF SUPPRESSION
BEGINS AGAIN.

MY BIG EMOTIONS HAD
TWO SETTINGS
UNTIL RECENTLY:
SHUT DOWN
OR EXPLODING OUT.
FINDING NEW WAYS OF
FULLY EXPRESSING MYSELF
HAS BEEN RATHER
UNCOMFORTABLE
BUT I'M REACHING NEW
DEPTHS THAT WERE
PREVIOUSLY
UNATTAINABLE AND
BURIED AWAY.

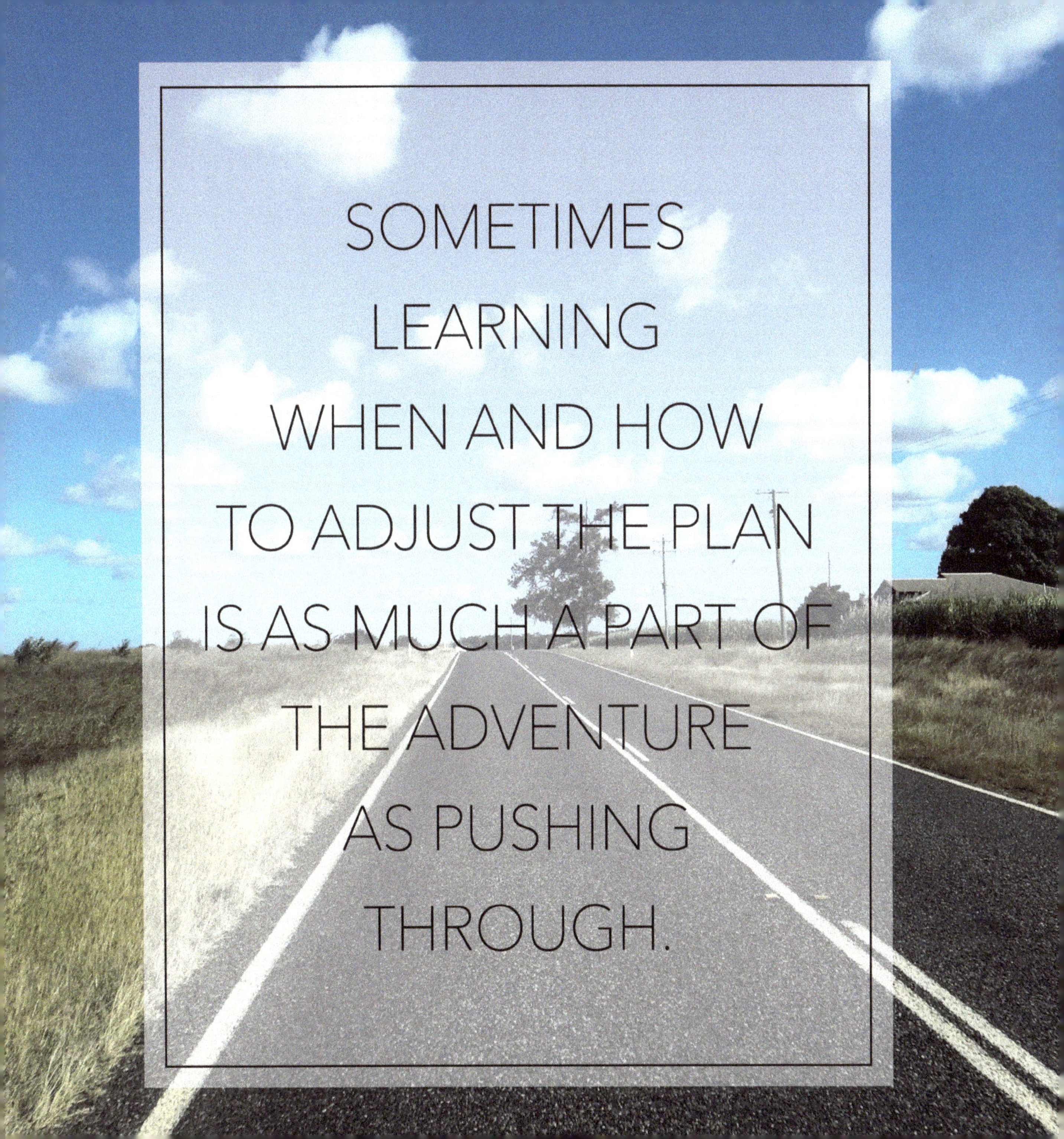

SOMETIMES LEARNING WHEN AND HOW TO ADJUST THE PLAN IS AS MUCH A PART OF THE ADVENTURE AS PUSHING THROUGH.

I'M LEARNING THAT
CELEBRATING AND
REWARDING PROGRESS
IS EQUALLY (IF NOT MORE)
IMPORTANT IN MY PROCESS
OF ACHIEVING GOALS
AS THE RESULTS.
PLUS THE PROCESS IS
FAR MORE FUN THAT WAY.

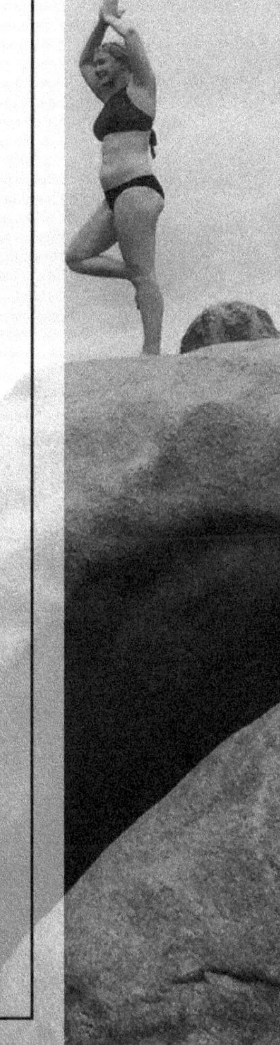

MY WELLBEING CONSISTS OF A ROUTINE
OF ACTIONS THAT I'VE LEARNED THROUGH
TRIAL AND ERROR ARE REQUIRED
IN ORDER FOR ME TO FUNCTION,
BUT WITH LITTLE ROOM FOR EXPANSION.
DESPITE KNOWING THEIR PURPOSE,
I END UP RESENTING THE STRUCTURES
AND AS SOON AS THEY ARE NO LONGER
ABSOLUTELY NECESSARY,
I CRASH AND BURN.
FUN AND ADVENTURE ARE RESERVED AS
BRIBERY FOR "GOOD" BEHAVIOUR.
SO I'VE DECIDED TO REFRAME MY
RELATIONSHIP TO WELLBEING FROM A
SURVIVAL KIT TO A THRIVING FOUNDATION,
WITH FUN AND ADVENTURE AS THE
KEYSTONES.

I AM VERY GOOD AT
TRYING NEW THINGS.
MY NATURAL CURIOSITY AND
VARIED SKILLSET MAKE IT EASY
TO LIVE LIFE WITH
A BEGINNER'S MINDSET.
I'M WORKING ON UTILIZING
THAT INNATE TENDENCY AS A
FOUNDATION FOR
BUILDING LONG-TERM
COMMITMENTS.

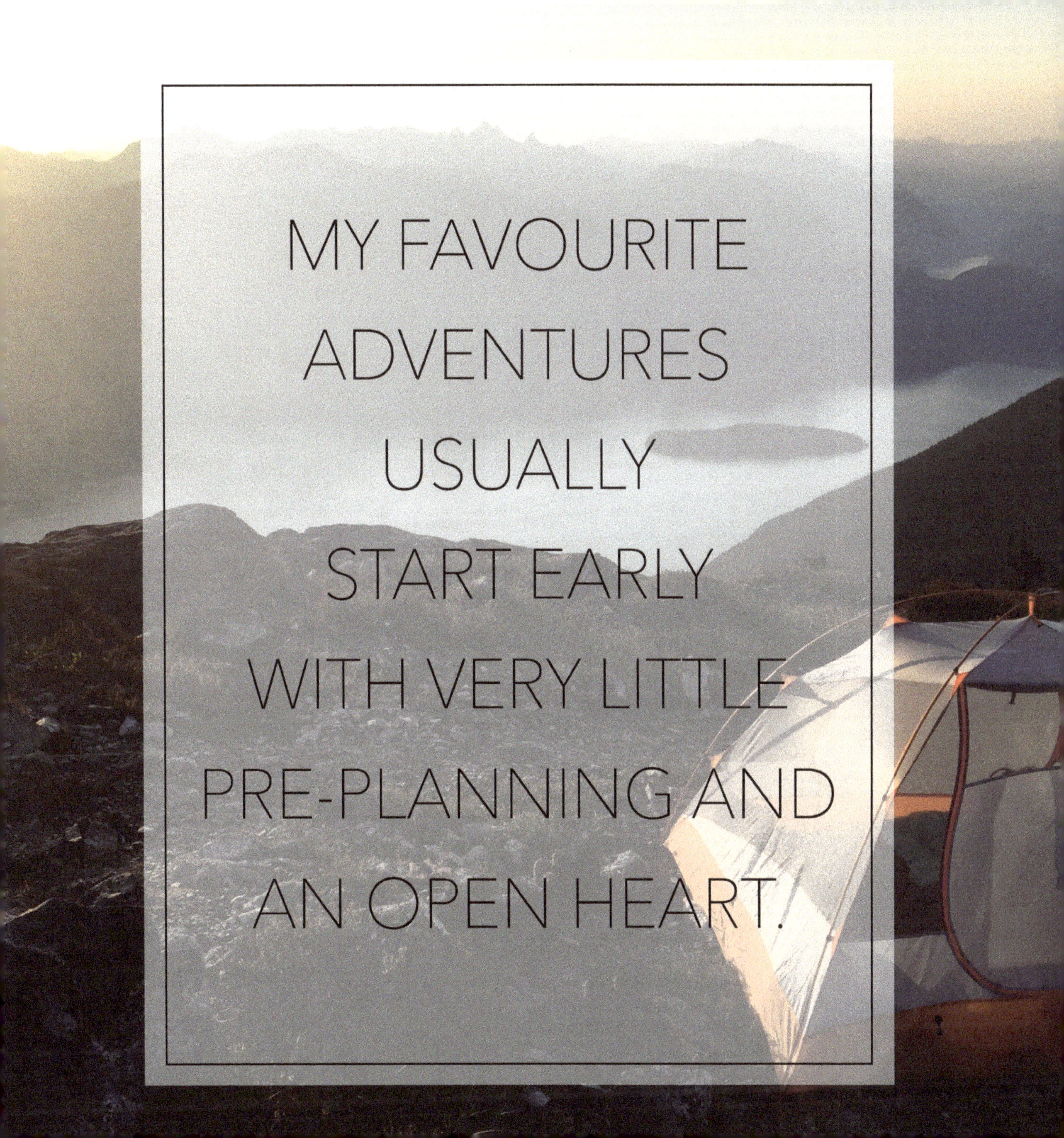

MY FAVOURITE
ADVENTURES
USUALLY
START EARLY
WITH VERY LITTLE
PRE-PLANNING AND
AN OPEN HEART.

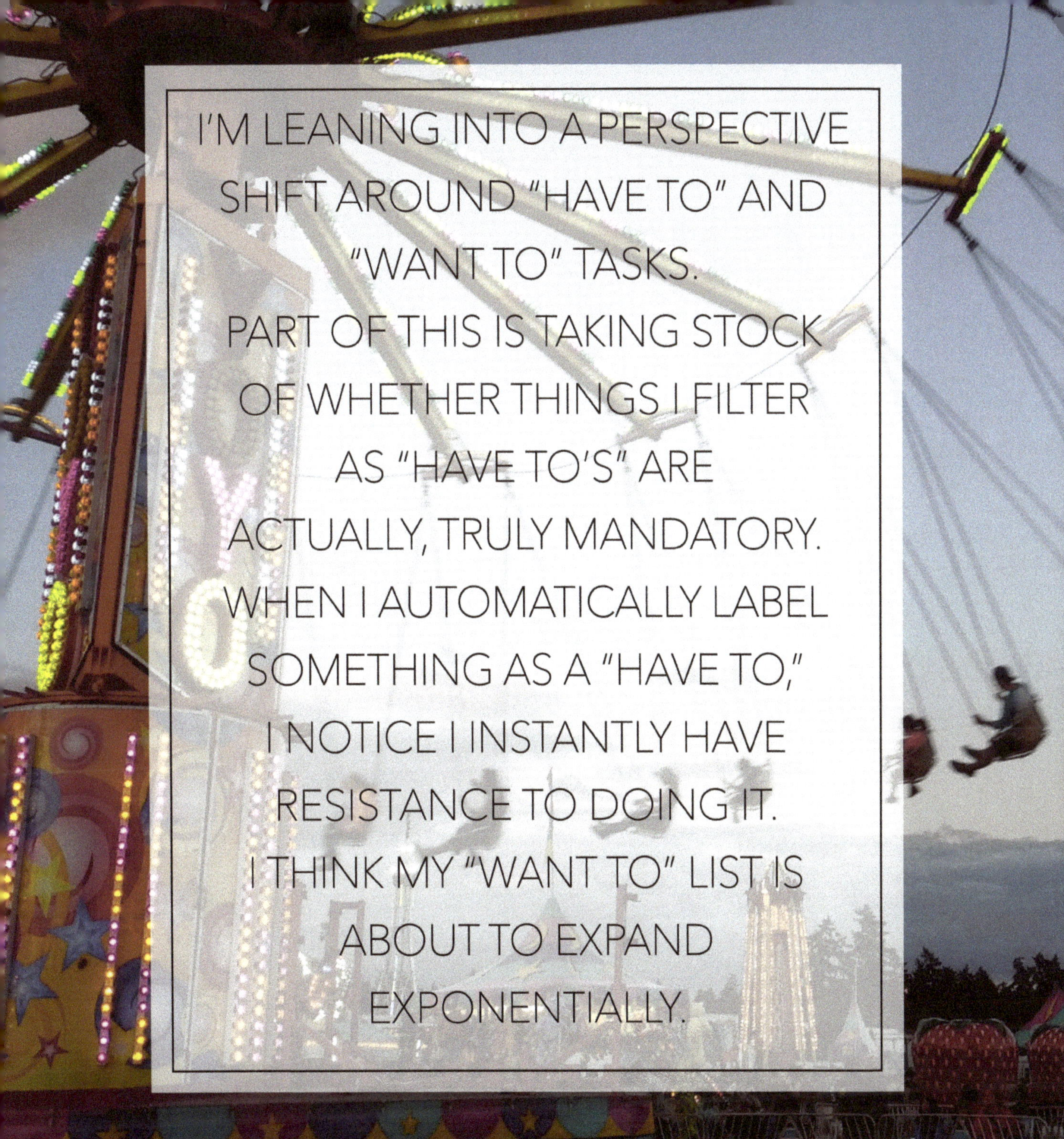

I'M LEANING INTO A PERSPECTIVE
SHIFT AROUND "HAVE TO" AND
"WANT TO" TASKS.
PART OF THIS IS TAKING STOCK
OF WHETHER THINGS I FILTER
AS "HAVE TO'S" ARE
ACTUALLY, TRULY MANDATORY.
WHEN I AUTOMATICALLY LABEL
SOMETHING AS A "HAVE TO,"
I NOTICE I INSTANTLY HAVE
RESISTANCE TO DOING IT.
I THINK MY "WANT TO" LIST IS
ABOUT TO EXPAND
EXPONENTIALLY.

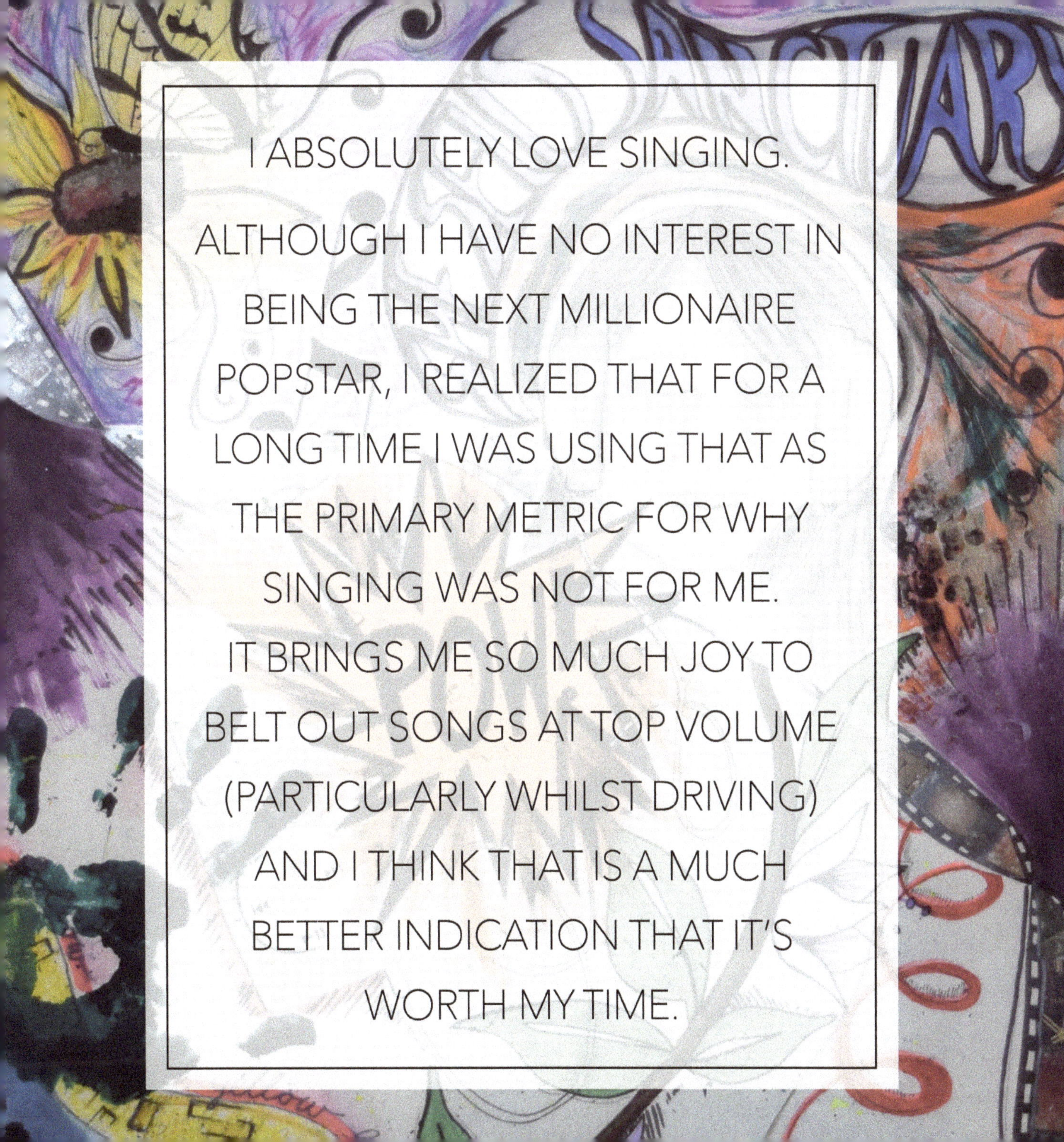

I ABSOLUTELY LOVE SINGING.

ALTHOUGH I HAVE NO INTEREST IN BEING THE NEXT MILLIONAIRE POPSTAR, I REALIZED THAT FOR A LONG TIME I WAS USING THAT AS THE PRIMARY METRIC FOR WHY SINGING WAS NOT FOR ME.

IT BRINGS ME SO MUCH JOY TO BELT OUT SONGS AT TOP VOLUME (PARTICULARLY WHILST DRIVING) AND I THINK THAT IS A MUCH BETTER INDICATION THAT IT'S WORTH MY TIME.

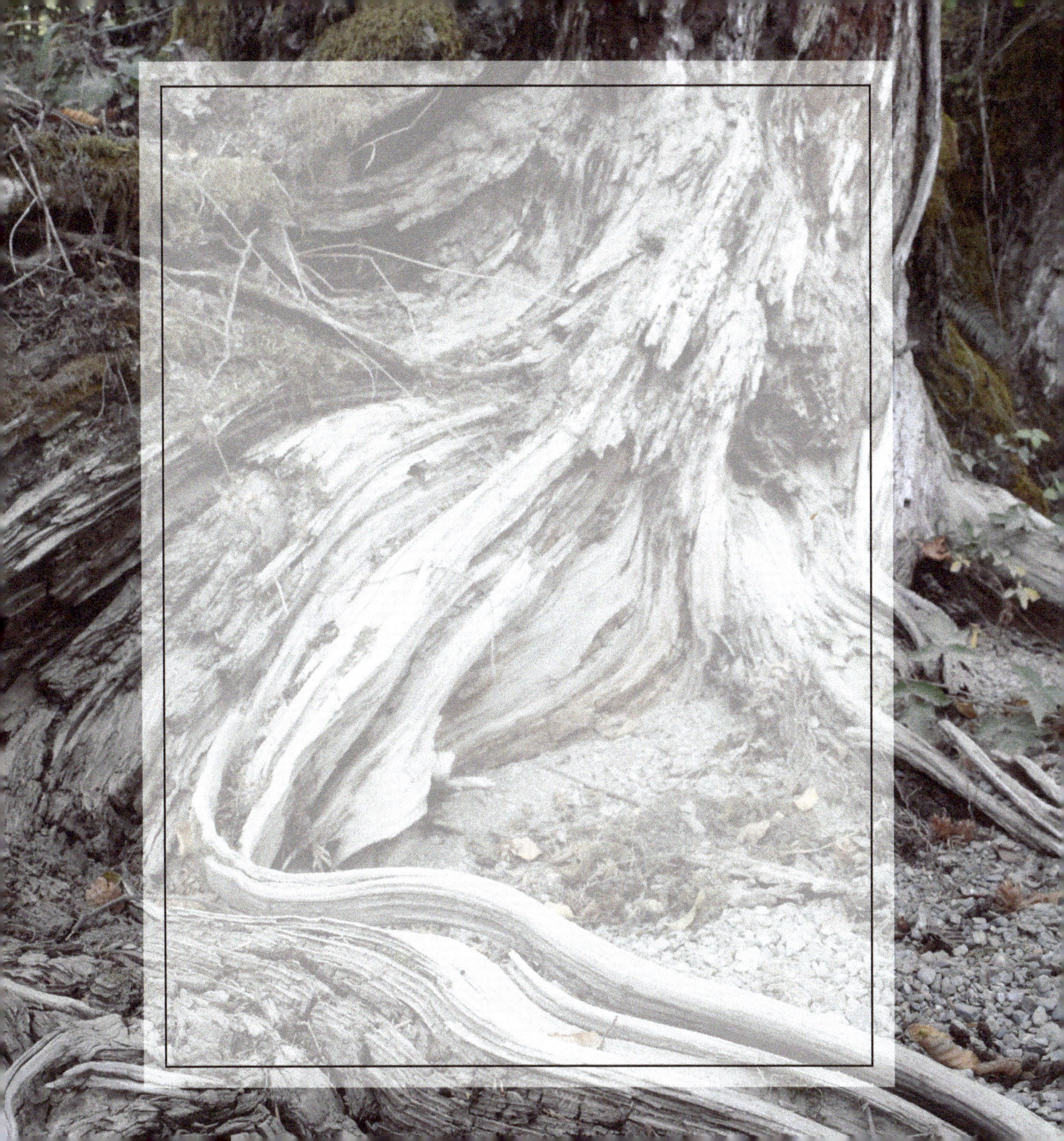

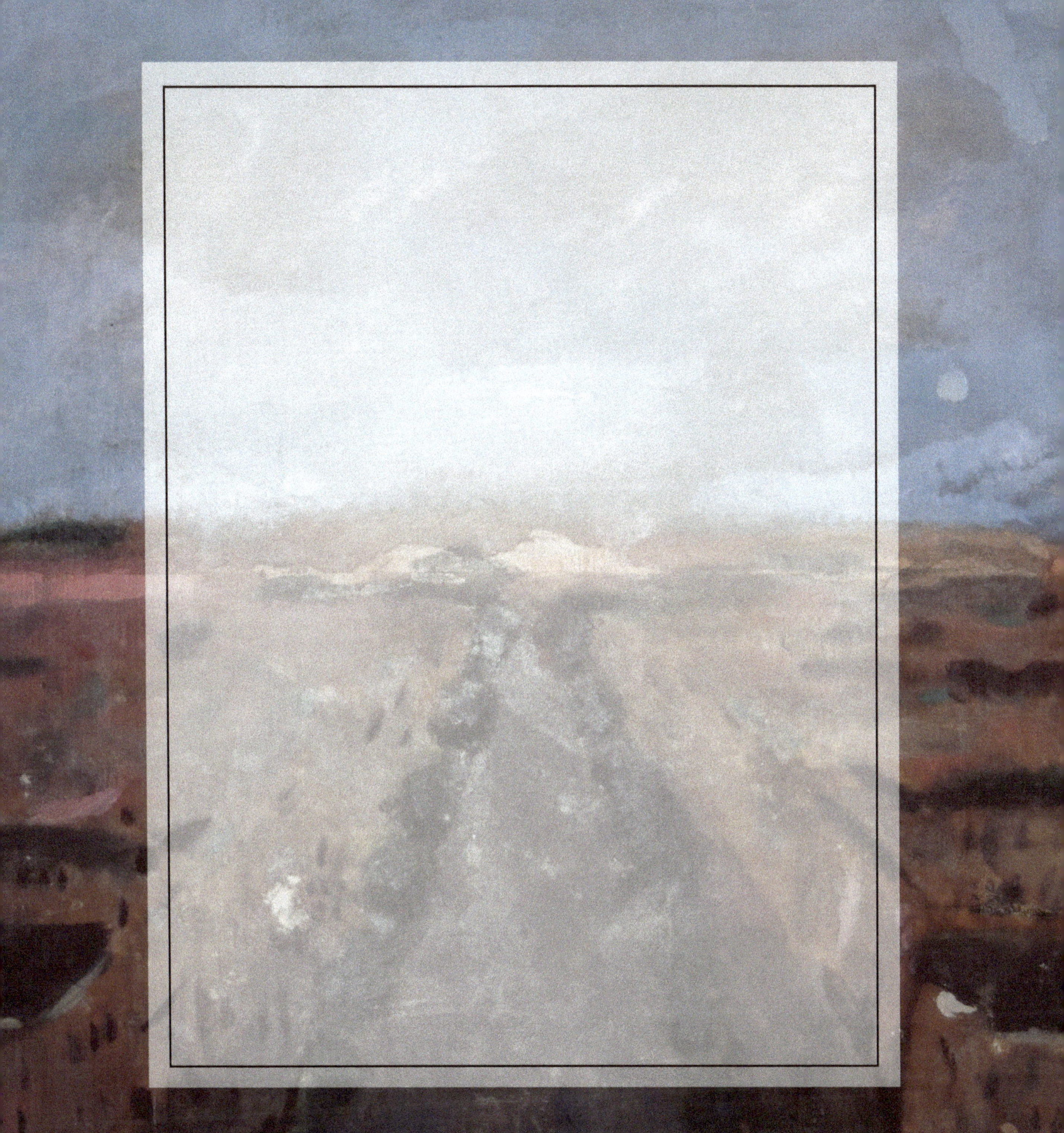

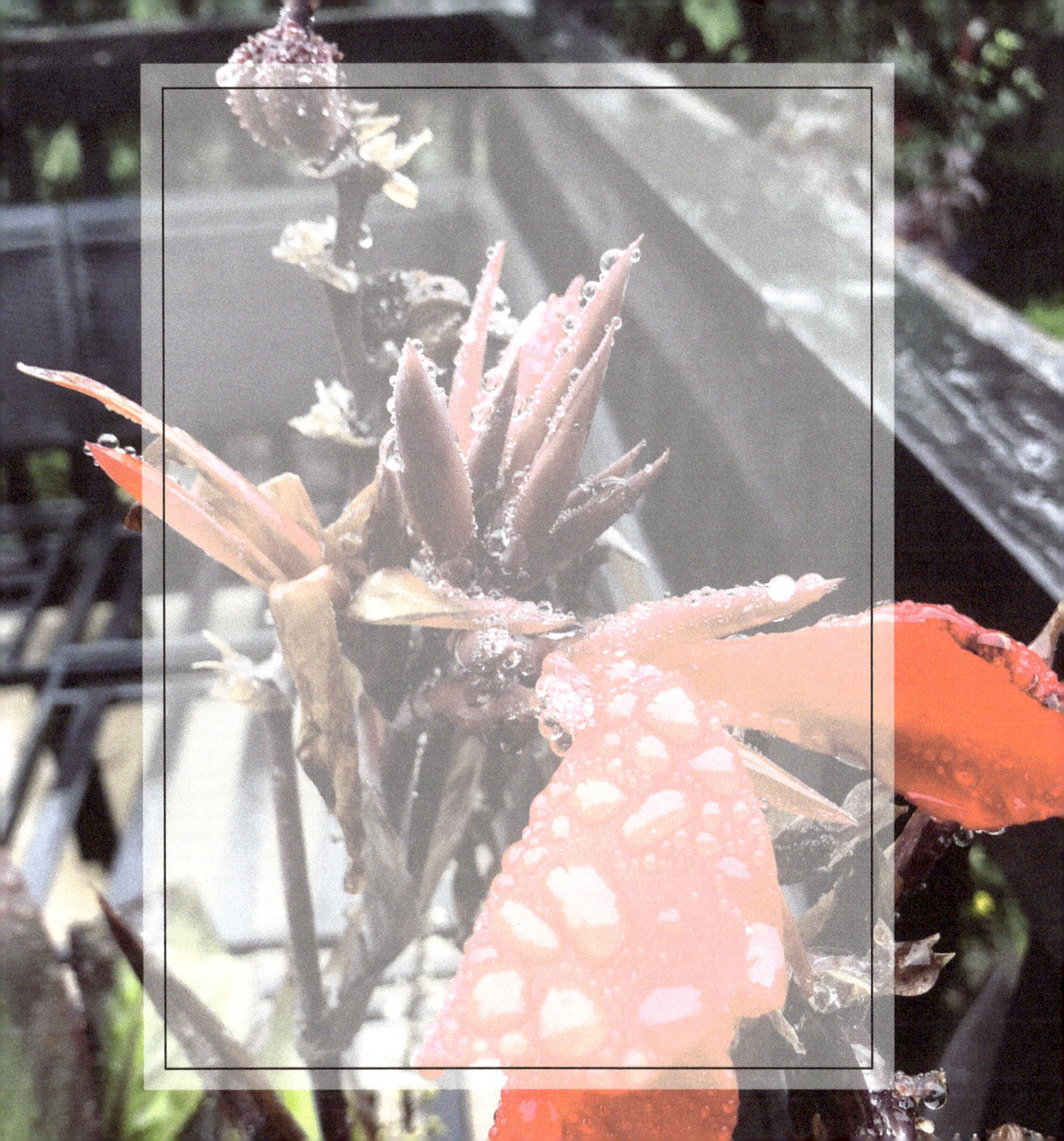

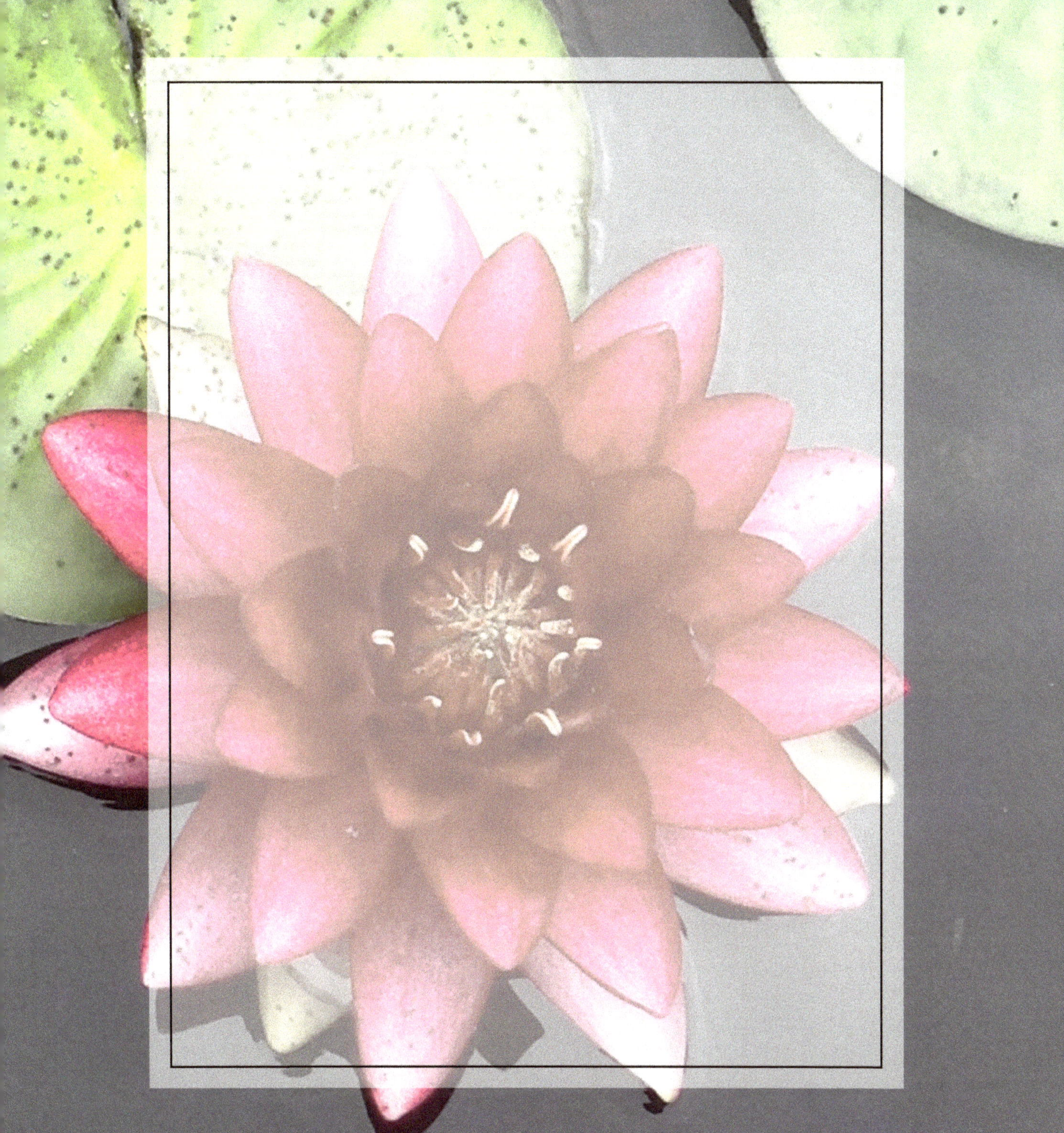

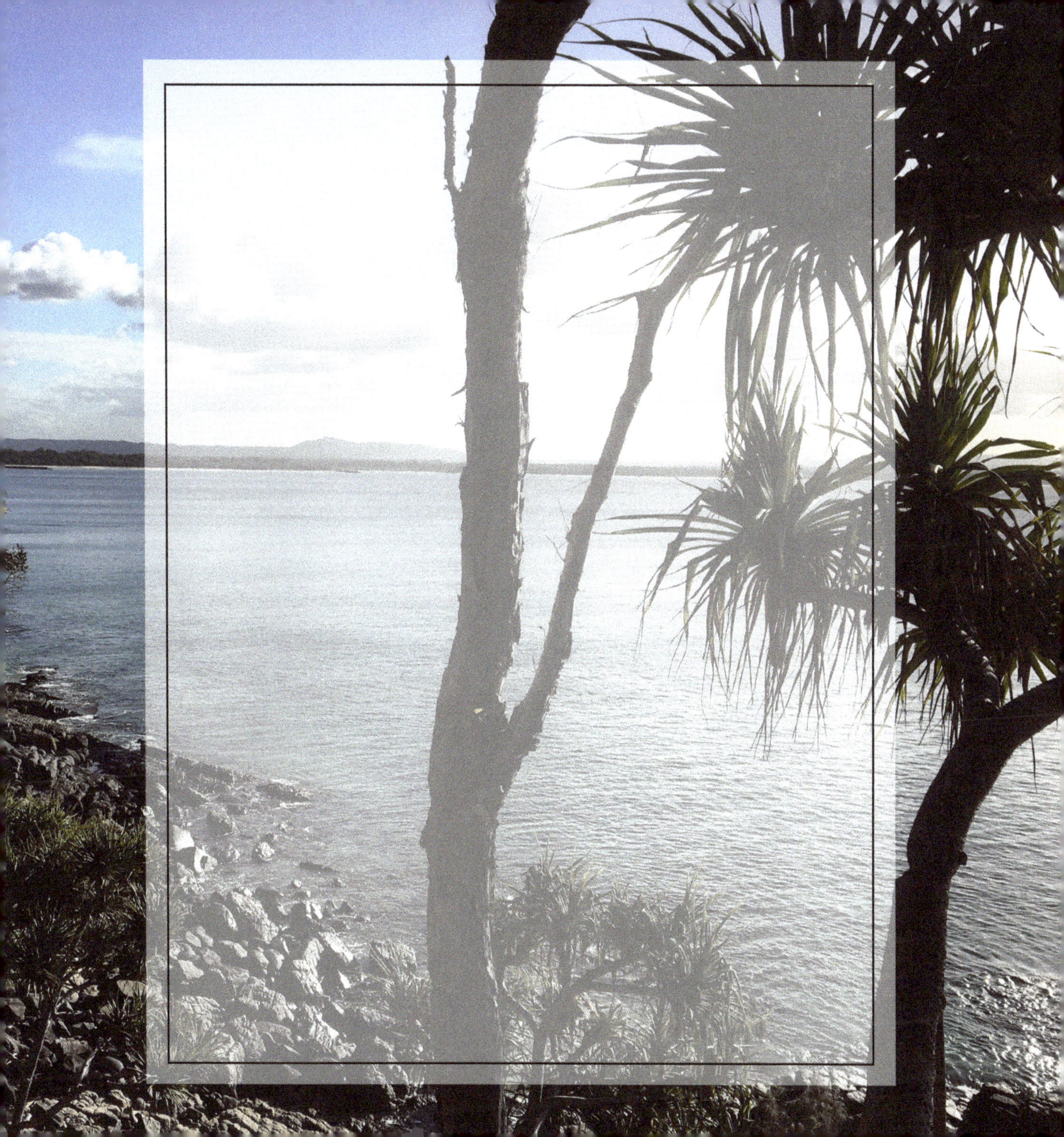

ACKNOWLEDGEMENT
IS SO IMPORTANT.
WHEN I'M HAVING A HARD TIME
FINDING ANYTHING TO
ACKNOWLEDGE MYSELF FOR,
IT HELPS TO LOOK AT
PEOPLE I ADMIRE
AND ACKNOWLEDGE THEM
INSTEAD.
EVEN IF THEY NEVER SEE IT,
THE PROCESS GIVES ME
SOMETHING TO ASPIRE TO.

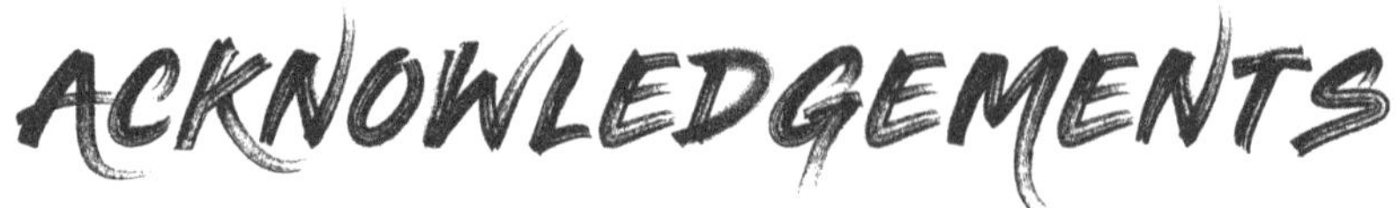

I acknowledge every person who has encouraged me in and contributed to my creativity at some point, in any small way. I also acknowledge every person who was discouraging, as they are ultimately who this book was written for. I sincerely hope you find your own creative journey and expression in your own time.

Thank you to Michelle for the continual creative kicks in the ass and for modelling the embodiment of authentic self-expression.

Thank you Alex, Lindsey and the Tiny Book Course team for the structure and enthusiastic inspiration to finish and publish this book, as well as the excellent music playlists.

Thank you Dana, Jen, Jenn, Mike and Alex for always being a hell-yes support system in everything I do.

Thank you to my life coach Tamara for being the backbone to a lot of the realizations included in this book – you are pure heart and magic.

Finally, thank you to my family for instilling in me that I'm never stuck and I can be whoever I want to be. I love you.

ABOUT THE AUTHOR

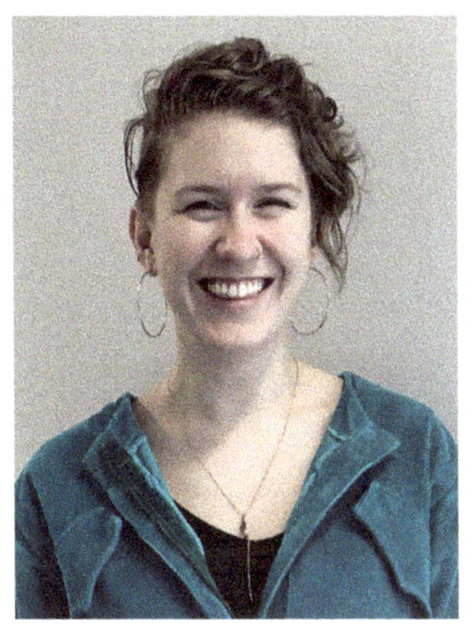

Jessica Blue is a visual artist and life coach with a day job in TV and Film. She exudes colour in everything, from her hair to her fashion to her approaches on problem solving. She holds a Bachelor's degree from The University of Victoria in Visual Arts and Computer Science, and is a graduate of the Accomplishment Coaching Coach Training Program.

With her combined degree in art and tech, Jessica is uniquely aware of the challenges of finding and expressing creativity in a world that values productivity and efficiency over artistry. Her mission is to empower anyone (including herself) who's ever uttered the phrase "I'm not creative" to find their own passionate exploration of what creativity means for them.

Clients have praised her creative inspiration, her authenticity and curiosity, and her endlessly buoyant energy.

Jessica currently lives on the traditional territories of the Coast Salish peoples, colonially known as Vancouver, Canada.

To learn more, visit her website at http://blankcanvasproject.ca